STEVE WAUGH
CAPTAIN'S DIARY 2002

STEVE WAUGH

CAPTAIN'S DIARY 2002

HarperSports

An imprint of HarperCollins*Publishers*

Harper*Sports*
An imprint of HarperCollins*Publishers*, Australia

First published in Australia in 2002
by HarperCollins*Publishers* Pty Limited
ABN 36 009 913 517
A member of HarperCollins*Publishers* (Australia) Pty Limited Group
www.harpercollins.com.au

HarperCollins*Publishers*
25 Ryde Road, Pymble, Sydney NSW 2073, Australia
31 View Road, Glenfield, Auckland 10, New Zealand
77–85 Fulham Palace Road, London W6 8JB, United Kingdom
Hazelton Lanes, 55 Avenue Road, Suite 2900, Toronto, Ontario M5R 3L2
and 1995 Markham Road, Scarborough, Ontario M1B 5M8, Canada
10 East 53rd Street, New York NY 10022, USA

Waugh, Steve, 1965- .
  Captain's diary 2002.
  ISBN 0 7322 7558 X.
  1. Waugh, Steve, 1965- – Diaries. 2. Cricket captains –
  Australia – Biography. 3. Cricket players – Australia –
  Biography. 4. Cricket – Australia. I. Title.
796.358092

Produced by Geoff Armstrong
Cover design: Nine Hundred VC
Internal design and layout: Graeme Jones

Photographs by Steve Waugh and Getty Images as credited. Photos on page 15 (Matthew Hayden and
Justin Langer, third Test v South Africa, Sydney, January 2002), page 33 (Steve Waugh during the 2001–02
VB Series), page 81 (Adam Gilchrist in South Africa, 2002), page 193 (Shane Warne, Glenn McGrath,
Steve Waugh and Ricky Ponting at the 2002 Laureus World Sports Awards), page 213 (Steve Waugh batting
for Kent, August 2002) and page 233 (Steve Waugh waits to return to the crease after retiring hurt while
playing for Kent v Leicestershire, August 2002) all Getty Images.

Printed and bound in Australia by Griffin Press on 100gsm Matt Art

6 5 4 3 2 1   02 03 04 05

Contents

Acknowledgments

I AM VERY GRATEFUL FOR all the help I've received in developing this book. I especially appreciate the help of my wife Lynette and children Rosalie, Austin and Lillian. Their support and love during a period of my cricket life that was exciting but — more than once — somewhat stressful, was total and so important to me.

Special thanks to the guys in the Australian squads (and their wives, partners and friends) for their continued support, for letting me describe their on-field performances and off-field events, and for allowing my camera into our dressing-rooms and other places. I also appreciate the help of the people around me who sometimes took my camera to take photographs amid the change-room celebrations and elsewhere. Thanks, too, to everyone at the Australian Cricket Board and the Australian Cricketers' Association, plus my management team at Duet and all my sponsors who have backed me throughout the past 12 months.

This book marks 10 years working with Geoff Armstrong, who has edited and helped produce every one of my books since *Steve Waugh's Ashes Diary* hit the bookstores in 1993. I appreciate his knowledge of cricket and the book-making business, plus his professionalism and total support.

Many of the photographs in *Captain's Diary 2002* are from the superb resources of Getty Images, and — as has been the case for many books now — I am grateful for their skill and help. The book also needed the legendary efforts of Graeme Jones, who designed and produced the final pages with style and at astonishing speed. Other important people in the publishing process were cover designer Chris Magus, the Queen of commas, Sarah Shrubb, and the ever-amazing Ian Russell, who has so many cricket statistics in his head that he'll overdose one day. And, of course, I must thank the people at HarperCollins for once again giving me the opportunity to produce a cricket diary.

Steve Waugh
September 2002

Prelude
by Geoff Armstrong

BY ANY MEASURE, 2001 WAS a memorable year for the Australian cricket team. It wasn't just that the team usually won that impressed; it was also the way those victories were gained. As a group, they were relentless, always aggressive, sensible, prepared to gamble, believers in a cause. Rarely, if ever, has a group of athletes been so united by collective self-belief, so confident that each of their comrades had total faith in them, and cared about them, that their leaders had faith in them, and cared about them. Their skipper was a man who appeared to have worked out the game of cricket — and what it took to succeed in big-time sport — as well as anyone in the long history of the game. His good fortune was to be working with a coach who matched his enthusiasm and perception, and even outdid him for innovative thought. The team became a reflection of their zeal.

The Australian Test XI's 2001 started with an emphatic victory over the West Indies in the New Year's Test at the SCG, to complete a 5–0 series clean sweep. It was Australia's 15th Test-match victory in a row, an astonishing sequence four better than had ever been achieved in Test history. After dominating the Carlton & United one-day series, the team went to India, to lose one of the most dramatic and thrilling series ever played. The first Test in Mumbai was won in style by 10 wickets, and after Steve Waugh enforced the follow-on in the second Test in Kolkata, it seemed that match would go the same way. Instead, VVS Laxman and Rahul Dravid batted throughout the fourth day, and then the off-spinner Harbhajan Singh bowled the locals to only the third Test victory ever won by a team that had been obliged to follow on. Straight after, in Chennai, India won again, this time by two wickets, after another exciting contest dominated by Harbhajan, who took 15 wickets in the Test, giving him 32 for the series. Australia's batting mainstay was Matthew Hayden, who scored 549 runs, including one double century, one single century and two fifties. Glenn McGrath (17 wickets) and Jason Gillespie (13) were Australia's leading bowlers, while Adam Gilchrist and Steve Waugh also scored centuries.

Straight after, the Australians won a one-day competition in India — no mean trick — by taking three of five games, including the last two. To do this so soon after such a gut-wrenching setback in the Test matches was a gallant achievement, especially for the players involved in both campaigns. After a seven-week break it was on to England, where the one-day team was superb in a tri-series that also involved England and Pakistan, and the Test XI retained the Ashes in exhilarating style. Waugh's men won four Tests and lost only at Headingley, after the home side successfully chased what with hindsight was probably an overly generous last-day target. Like Laxman and Dravid in Kolkata, Mark Butcher produced the innings of his life to get England home; it was if playing the Australians brought out the very best in the more audacious of opponents. McGrath took 32 wickets for the series, one more than Shane Warne. Steve Waugh averaged 107 with the bat, Mark Waugh 86, Damien Martyn 76.40, Gilchrist 68. Observers such as Ian Botham suggested Waugh's side was better than Bradman's Invincibles, while the captain himself could relish the fact that he was now the only man to have been a part of four separate Australian teams that had won Ashes series in England.

Test Cricket in 2001

In 2001, no team appeared in more Test matches than Australia, who played 14 Tests, one more than India, England and South Africa. In contrast, Pakistan played only six, Bangladesh eight. Perhaps the number of matches the Australians played was a factor in their slow start to the 2001–02 Australian season, though rain was mostly responsible for all three Tests of the series against the New Zealand Black Caps in November–December being drawn. (Another explanation was that the Black Caps under Stephen Fleming were a very tough team to beat — they won three of eight Tests in 2001, and lost only once.)

Even with these stalemates, Australia's eight wins in 2001 was matched only by Sri Lanka, who lost five times to Australia's three. South Africa had six wins and three losses, two of those defeats being to Steve Waugh's team in December. Going into that series in Australia, which was advertised as a battle for the world championship, South Africa had lost only six Tests, while winning 25 of 45, since the two sides had last met, in 1997–98. And one of those losses had only come about after a declaration from captain Hansie Cronje had set up a Test at Centurion Park for England. They were not an easy team to conquer.

A study of the best performers for 2001 reveals just how many members of the Australian team had 'career' years. Take, for example, the year's batting statistics. Only eight batsmen played more than 10 Test innings and averaged 60 or more per innings — Zimbabwe's Andy Flower (89.90), Pakistan's Inzamam-ul-Haq (70.28), South Africa's Jacques Kallis (70.00), Damien Martyn (65.80), West Indies' Brian Lara (63.94), Matthew Hayden (63.22), India's Sachin Tendulkar (62.68) and New Zealand's Mark Richardson (60.27). Hayden was the leading run-getter for the 12 months in Test cricket, scoring 1391 runs, the third-highest aggregate ever achieved by a Test batsman in one calendar year. Other batsmen to score 1000 Test runs in 2001 were Lara, Kallis and Herschelle Gibbs of South Africa, Sri Lanka's Mahela Jayawardene and the incomparable Tendulkar. Hayden's five centuries were the most hit by a batsman, one clear of his colleagues, Justin Langer and Steve Waugh, and Jayawardene. The highest score of the year was made by VVS Laxman — 281 against the Australians in Kolkata.

It is in the area of rapid scoring that the Australians come into their own. Adam Gilchrist might have 'only' made 870 runs, including three centuries, but he got them at the exceptional scoring rate of 81.92 runs per hundred balls faced. The only other player to score more than 260 runs and have a scoring rate over 70 was Ricky Ponting (772 runs at 70.37 runs per hundred balls). In all, 36 batsmen scored more than 500 runs during the year, but only eight did so at a scoring rate faster than 60 runs per hundred balls. Of those eight, five were Aussies: Gilchrist, Ponting, Hayden, Martyn and Michael Slater (the other three were Laxman, Jayawardene and Sri Lankan captain Sanath Jayasuriya). Gilchrist also completed 57 wicketkeeping dismissals, the most by any wicketkeeper during the 12 months. Ponting, with 25, took the most catches by a non-keeper, one clear of Mark Waugh.

The leading wicket-taker in Test cricket in 2001 was Sri Lanka's remarkable Muttiah Muralitharan, who took 80 wickets, 12 more than Glenn McGrath. Muralitharan played in two fewer Tests than McGrath, but bowled 1180 more deliveries. Harbhajan Singh was third, with 60 dismissals (including 8–84 in Chennai, the best innings analysis returned during the year). Other notable Australian performances came from Shane Warne (58 wickets in 13 Tests) and Jason Gillespie (47 wickets in 13). Sri Lanka's Chaminda Vaas (58), South Africa's Shaun Pollock (55) and England's Darren Gough (45) were the only bowlers besides Muralitharan, McGrath, Warne and Gillespie to take more than 40 wickets.

One-day International cricket in 2001

The team with the best win-rate in one-day international cricket was Australia, who lost only three times — twice to India and once to Pakistan — in 21 matches. However, South Africa weren't far behind, winning 17 of 21. Sri Lanka won the most matches: 22 of 34.

Six batsmen scored more than 1000 runs in one-day cricket during the year, all from Zimbabwe (who played the most matches, 37) or Sri Lanka (who played the second-most). Sachin Tendulkar scored 904 runs for the year in 16 innings (the six with more than 1000 runs all played more than 30), at an average of 69.53. That average was excellent, but not as high as Mark Waugh's, who scored 809 runs at 80.90. The top five averages of those batsmen to score more than 200 ODI runs during the year belonged to Mark Waugh, Tendulkar, Damien Martyn (69.50), South Africa's Boeta Dippenaar (68.00) and Australia's Michael Bevan (64.55). Both Tendulkar and Mark Waugh hit four centuries, but it was the Australian who made the highest score of the year — 173 in the second final of the Carlton & United Series, against the West Indies at the MCG. Of the six batsmen to score 100 runs or more at better than a run a ball, two were Aussies — Andrew Symonds and Ian Harvey.

Muttiah Muralitharan, as prolific in the shorter version of the game as he is in Tests, captured the most one-day wickets in 2001 — 56 at 18.19 — ahead of his compatriot Chaminda Vaas (who, among his 42 wickets, took a world record 8–19 against Zimbabwe in Colombo) and Zimbabwe's Heath Streak. Pakistan captain Waqar Younis took 41 wickets for the year, one less than Vaas and Streak, in eight fewer matches than the Sri Lankan and 10 fewer than the Zimbabwean. Of all bowlers to take more than 10 ODI wickets, only Pakistan's Shoaib Akhtar (17 wickets at 17.64) had a lower bowling average than Muralitharan. The leading Australian wicket-takers were, as usual, Glenn McGrath and Shane Warne, but while the champion leg-spinner took more wickets (32 to 29), the great fast man was probably superior. McGrath's wickets came at a cost of 23.28 runs per wicket, two and a half runs less than Warne, while he conceded 4.11 runs per over, with Warne going for just under five. Both played 18 matches. These economy rates lag behind Shaun Pollock and Muralitharan, who of mainstream bowlers were toughest to score off. Pollock conceded 3.18 runs per over in taking 27 wickets in 21 games, and Muralitharan took his wickets in 33 matches while conceding 3.3 runs per over. Behind the stumps, Adam Gilchrist,

Mark Boucher and Ridley Jacobs completed the most dismissals (each 34), the Australian playing in one fewer match than the South African and seven fewer than the West Indian.

Steve Waugh in 2001 ... and beyond

Of course, cricket statistics don't always paint an accurate picture, and it would be a foolish critic who relied on them totally to form his or her opinions. But these numbers do reveal how influential many members of the Australian teams — Test and one-day — were through 2001. They could hardly have expected that, come 2002, for some of them things might suddenly turn for the worse.

Steve Waugh would certainly have been in this group. When he became Test captain at the beginning of 1999 his Test-match record looked like this:

Tests	Innings	NO	Runs	HS	Ave	100	50
111	177	34	7213	200	50.44	17	40

From there to the end of the calendar year 2000, a run of 20 Tests, Waugh's Test résumé improved:

Tests	Innings	NO	Runs	HS	Ave	100	50
131	200	39	8581	200	50.77	23	42

Eight Tests on — one against the West Indies at the SCG, three in India and four in England (Waugh missed the fourth Test of this Ashes series through injury) — and the record now appeared this way:

Tests	Innings	NO	Runs	HS	Ave	100	50
139	220	41	9286	200	51.87	27	42

A feature of these stats — besides the steadily growing batting average — is the fact that in a period when Waugh scored 10 centuries, he made only two scores between 50 and 99. One of these was an unbeaten 72 when he ran out of partners in Antigua in 1999. Ironically, Waugh had made 96, his ninth Test ninety, in his final Test as vice-captain, at the Sydney Cricket Ground in the fifth Ashes Test of 1998–99. And he would make two more scores between 50 and 99 in the first half of the Australian summer of 2001–02 — both of these innings ending when he was run out.

Unfortunately, those two half-centuries were Waugh's only significant contributions with the bat to Australia's first five Tests of 2001–02. By the end of the year his Test batting average had 'dipped' to 50.94, and for the first time in almost a decade the Australian captain heard whispers from critics, who brought up his age (36) and questioned his future. The fact that by year's end he had led Australia in 33 Tests for 23 victories (and five draws and five losses) — the best success rate of any permanent Australian captain bar Warwick Armstrong, who won eight of 10 straight after World War I — was, in the eyes of some, his saving grace.

Waugh's record in one-day cricket since he became captain was as impressive as his Test results, perhaps even more so. Before the 2002 VB Series one-day competition, the team had won 63 from 106 since he first became skipper in 1997, having lost eight of its first 10 under Waugh's captaincy, and 11 of its first 17. They'd won 37 from 48 (with one tie) since the 1999 World Cup. That tournament, when Australia prevailed in each of their last seven matches to claim the trophy, was something of a watershed for Waugh's one-day career, as captain and batsman. Before the '99 World Cup, his career ODI batting average was 31.01; by the end of 2001 it had risen to 32.95. As New Year's Day 2002 dawned, Waugh could look back on a year when he averaged 48.50 in one-day internationals.

Six weeks later, it appeared to most people — including the Australian selectors — that his one-day international career was over . . .

Captain's Diary 2002

This is the ninth Steve Waugh cricket diary. When this publishing assignment began — with Australia's 1993 tour of England — the task was to cover an overseas tour or tournament: the '93 Ashes tour, then South Africa in 1994, the West Indies in 1995, the 1996 World Cup, England in 1997. However, as each year's cricket calendar expanded, at the same time as the status of both the Australian team and Waugh himself grew, it seemed that each year threw up new adventures and greater achievements. It wasn't enough to look at one tour — for 1998–99, we had not just the team's fantastic World Cup triumph, but also the Commonwealth Games, an important Ashes series in Australia, a West Indies tour and the Cup. Twelve months later, the Test and one-day teams went on their famous 'streaks' (a world record 13 one-day internationals unbeaten, and an unbroken 10-game winning run in Tests, which continued on to 16 in 2000–01), so the diary was in Sri Lanka,

Zimbabwe, Australia, New Zealand, South Africa and finally at Colonial Stadium for the first ever indoor one-day internationals. The year 2001 gave us another successful Ashes tour, this time with the new angle of Waugh as captain, but before that India and Australia played out that wonderful three-Test series, followed by an exciting one-day competition. So *Ashes Diary 2001* also featured highlights from the team's seven weeks on the subcontinent.

So much of this has been about success. Even when the team didn't win it all — as at the 1996 World Cup or in India in 2001 — it found itself involved in brilliant cricket, playing a major part in stories that deserved to be told. For nine years, Steve Waugh has written tales of thrills and triumph.

On one level, that trend continues in the pages that follow. The Australian Test team through the first three months of 2002 proved far too good for South Africa, reaffirming their status as cricket's No. 1 team. Two months later, in Monte Carlo at the Laureus World Sports Awards, Waugh's men were recognised as the finest team in all sport. However, this accolade came after the captain had been omitted from the Australian one-day squad, after his team had failed to reach the finals of the VB Series. Consequently, this book is a story of success *and* setback.

Captain's Diary 2002 covers the period from January to August, from the conclusion to the Australia–South Africa Test series in Australia to Waugh's stint playing county cricket for Kent. The Test skipper found himself in England searching for all-important time in the middle, as he prepared for Australia's three-Test series against Pakistan and then a home Ashes series. The words come from Steve's pen, some of them having been adapted from columns that he wrote during the Australian season and the South African tour. Once again, he provides an insider's view of the team, how the issues of the day impact on the players, and how the joys of touring and winning bond them so closely together. But at the same time, he examines the reasons why his own cricket adventure has struck a detour.

Whether the decision to axe Steve Waugh as one-day captain was correct only time will tell. Certainly, the team without Steve Waugh got off to an impressive start under new captain Ricky Ponting, winning the first six of seven one-dayers in South Africa, before losing two of three matches against Pakistan in June. In my view, the selectors should be commended for their courage — there is no doubt that they must always be proactive — but I wonder if they have underestimated what a once-in-a-generation cricketer Steve Waugh is. Such players are not to be discarded rashly, because in cricket they are not easy to replace. It was worth the risk to drop Ian Healy from the one-day team in 1997, because in Adam Gilchrist Australian cricket had an accomplished replacement waiting for a chance. But when David Boon was jettisoned a couple of years earlier, there was no genuine No. 3 to replace him and the team suffered without him. Much has been made of the way the Liverpool and Manchester United football clubs have made a policy of moving on past champions at the first sign of wear, the logic being that in this way a team never grows old and stale. And certainly for Liverpool in the late 1970s and 1980s and for the current United team this worked well. However, to a large degree this success came about because in Bob Paisley (Liverpool) and Sir Alex Ferguson (Manchester United) these clubs had perceptive managers who nine times out of 10 were right when they decided a great player was done. Both managers also had the advantage of a huge transfer budget, so the best could be replaced by the best and mistakes could be made. The Australian cricket selectors have no such luxury.

For the moment, everyone with an interest in Australian cricket — selectors, fans, players, reporters, captains — is entitled to an opinion as to whether the selectors were right to make changes as they did. The pages that follow may help you shape yours.

Geoff Armstrong
Editor, Steve Waugh diaries 1993–2002
September 2002

PART 1

THE NEW YEAR'S TEST 2001–02

Another year. Practice in Sydney, New Year's Day 2002.

January 1

Sydney

IT'S BEEN A BIT WEIRD, the last few weeks, the last few months really. Since we retained the Ashes at The Oval, things haven't quite gone to plan. And yet as I write this, on the eve of the third Test against South Africa, with the series already wrapped up, 2–0, and my own batting form seemingly on the improve after an innings of 90 in Melbourne, I can't help thinking that everything is going to work out okay. Today at the Sydney Cricket Ground, the famous venue was covered in a smoky haze, a product of the bushfires that are blazing in and around my hometown, and as the guys came off the field it looked as if they were emerging from a cloud. For me, that image just about sums up how I feel about my first half of the season.

My troubles started when I suffered an episode of DVT Syndrome after our flight home from England. Tests showed that I had a massive haematoma, measuring 20cm by 10cm by 1.5cm deep, in my left calf,

NSW's Brett Lee is too classy for Andy Bichel of Queensland during a game of touch footy at practice on the eve of the third Test against South Africa.

which was a result of a major bleed sustained during my innings of 157 not out at The Oval in the fifth Test of the 2001 Ashes series. I knew that I had done some damage apart from the previously diagnosed serious double tear of the calf muscle, which I'd incurred during the third Test, at Trent Bridge, but thought that this new 'tweak' was only minor. But a combination of the internal bleeding and the enormous pressure from the cabin atmosphere caused a blood clot to develop, and as a consequence complete rest, blood-thinning injections and endless tablets were my preparation for the upcoming season. For six weeks I couldn't pick up a bat. After just one game in Sydney grade cricket, I was playing in a Test match against New Zealand, and not surprisingly I was a little rusty. However, by the end of that series — which ended square at 0–0 after too much rain and some feisty performances by the 'Black Caps' — I felt as if some form was coming back. This was especially so after the final day of the series, in Perth, when we had a shot at getting more than 400 in the fourth innings to win the match. Gilly was going along magnificently, at better than a run a ball, and I had reached 67 in support, when Daniel Vettori deflected a straight drive from our champion batsman-keeper onto the bowler's end stumps. I was a couple of metres out of my ground. But for that freak dismissal, I really think we would have won.

Our confrontations with the South Africans — first three Tests in Australia, then the VB one-day series which will also involve New Zealand, then three Tests and seven one-dayers in South Africa — have been promoted as a clash between the top two teams in the world. We went into the Test series here in Australia quietly confident, as we genuinely feel we have a psychological edge over them, but we knew that we'd have to pick up on how we'd played in the Trans-Tasman Tests. However optimistic we might have been, I'm not sure any of us could have imagined just how decisive our victories in the first two Tests would be, as so many guys in our squad suddenly produced a string of superb performances. Matthew Hayden and Justin Langer have been as prolific as any opening batting partnership in Test history. Glenn McGrath and Shane Warne have confirmed once again that they are two of the greatest bowlers ever to don a cricket boot. Damien Martyn has continued on from the Ashes series in England, and is now averaging well over 50 per innings in Test matches. Mark Waugh and Ricky Ponting have made some critical runs, Brett Lee has been a little inconsistent, but also quick and intimidating at times. Jason Gillespie bowled superbly in Adelaide, and when he was injured and had to miss the Boxing Day Test, Andy

Bichel came in and was just about our best bowler on what was a pretty flat wicket. Everywhere, our fielding and catching has been top class. If I had to pick one word to sum up our performances, I think I'd use 'relentless'.

After the Melbourne Test, South African captain Shaun Pollock was generous in his praise of our efforts. 'Their rating of the number one team is totally justified,' he said, when asked what he thought of the Australian team. 'We had high hopes when we came to Australia but at the end of the day we've been beaten by a better team. We have got a talented bunch but I don't think we did ourselves justice.'

When I was asked what might have been behind the South Africans' disappointing form, I replied, 'The intensity for the game was excellent. We have played good cricket, we've had them under pressure constantly and it's always hard to produce the goods in that situation. I'd like to think it was our good cricket that did it.

'Some of their batsmen haven't had a lot of experience at playing against this Australia side — coming up against guys like Glenn McGrath and Shane Warne at their best. Mentally that can wear you down a bit.'

Further emphasising our dominance over the Proteas is the decision made a couple of days back for their all-rounder Lance Klusener to go home. It seems like only yesterday he was slamming the world's best attacks all over the place during the 1999 World Cup. He has had a horror tour, which included a pair against NSW and a first-ball duck in the Melbourne Test, and he seems totally out of sorts. Usually, he is one of their major impact players. For him to admit he's not playing well enough and that he feels intimidated against us to the point that he doesn't know where his next run is coming from — I guess that shows we're doing something right.

Significantly, Klusener seems to have lost his 'tongue', which in the past has been one of his most powerful weapons. He's always been a talker, providing a running commentary that ranged from complimentary to derogatory, but always in a way that we consider part of the game. Playing against Lance Klusener is usually enjoyable, because you know you're in a contest. Sadly for him, during this series he's lost belief in his ability, and his lack of confidence and disheartened attitude towards us seems to have had a negative effect on the South African team.

My 90 in Melbourne came from 156 balls, and ended when I was run out. After starting shakily, I really felt a big score was coming — from 30 onwards I felt in complete control. It meant that I now have 10 Test nineties to my name, which puts me one clear of Michael Slater as the guy with the most scores between 90 and 99 in Test-match history. There are worse records I could hold.

The smoke that surrounds us in Sydney reminds me of India. It's not as bad now as it was two days ago, when it was choking, but with the bushfire forecasts grim it could be that we'll be playing the entire Test, which starts tomorrow, in a haze. Living as I do on the edge of bushland, and having seen first-hand the threat that bushfires can pose, I feel we have an obligation to play entertaining cricket, to provide a small diversion for the people who have been hurt by the fires.

That entertainment might include two champion leg-spinners bowling in tandem, though whether we go that way will depend on our final assessment of the Sydney wicket. Of course, Sydney has a history of favouring the slow bowlers, and Stuey MacGill has had great success here, but the pitch is certainly not the same as we've come to expect from the SCG. It's hard and has a nice grass cover. And we can't forget how well Bic bowled in Melbourne.

The final selection is going to be difficult, but I can't help thinking that it's a nice problem to have.

January 3

Sydney

**Australia v South Africa, Third Test Day One,
Sydney Cricket Ground**
Australia 5–308 (89.3 overs: JL Langer 126, ML Hayden 105) v South Africa

**Australia v South Africa, Third Test Day Two,
Sydney Cricket Ground**
Australia 554 (144.2 overs: DR Martyn 117; N Boje 4–63) v South Africa 4–93
(37 overs: GD McGrath 2–25, SCG MacGill 2–30)

FOR THE FIRST TWO DAYS of this Test we have been very much in the ascendancy. Once again, this all started through a brilliant effort by our

Mark Waugh batting on the first day of the third Test. Note the slightly eerie light, as the afternoon sun tries to shine through the smoky atmosphere created by Sydney's ugly bushfires.

BOTH PICS GETTY IMAGES

LEFT: **Justin Langer sweeps during his first-innings century, his fourth in his last seven Tests.**
BELOW: **Jacques Kallis, caught Gilchrist bowled MacGill, as South Africa's top order crumbles late on the second day.**

prolific opening bats, Justin Langer and Matthew Hayden, who batted through the first two sessions of the Test to add 219 for the first wicket. Both scored hundreds, as they compiled their fourth double century opening stand of the summer. By stumps, we had stumbled a little, to be 5–308, which we probably would have accepted at the start of play but not after our electrifying start. I was bowled by Pollock for 30, a frustrating out because I felt as if I was just beginning to settle in when I was dismissed and had all of tomorrow to look forward to. During my career I have prided myself on not being dismissed in the last half hour of play. An opportunity wasted is one you can never have back.

Today, the second day, Adam Gilchrist, Shane Warne and especially Damien Martyn played extremely well to get us all the way to 554. This was Marto's fourth hundred in 11 Tests since he came back into the side at the start of last year's Ashes series, and was a polished knock that reflected how confident and composed he now feels at this level.

The most amazing aspect of Marto's dig was the number of times he played the reverse sweep. This shows that he has the skill to be able to develop and execute the shot, and more importantly it reveals that he now has the confidence, poise and belief to do anything in Test cricket. I'm sure he will never look back again, because he knows now that he belongs at this level.

In reply, the South Africans were in big trouble at stumps, four wickets down and more than 450 behind. A lot now depends on their debutant Justin Ontong, who is 8 not out but must also be nervous because of the kerfuffle that followed his selection in their side. Apparently he is only playing because the head of the South African Cricket Board insisted he be picked so that the team would have its required quota of black or coloured players. I don't think it's for me to comment on the rights or wrongs of that policy — I really don't know all the issues involved — but I can say that Ontong seems a pretty good player.

Off the field, it was announced that the Australian cricket team has backed the NSW bushfires relief effort by donating 10 autographed cricket bats that will be auctioned over the internet. The proceeds will go to the Salvation Army's bushfire relief fund. It's been heartbreaking watching the fires cause their devastation over the past week and a half, and anything we can offer to help the affected communities rebuild their lives we are more than happy to do.

Let's Celebrate Two of the Best

The selection of Stuart MacGill in the Australian Test team is a topic that is always going to create headlines. The continued competition between he and Warney always seems to be turned into a fierce rivalry that projects them as enemies, which isn't true. Comparisons between the two are inevitable, at times rather tedious, but I guess they're newsworthy all the same.

Without doubt 'Magilla' would have already been a superstar in another era and even now there is still a possibility that will happen, for he has a natural gift that doesn't come along very often.

Warney, as we all know and have seen once again during this series against South Africa, is a genius, a once-in-a-lifetime phenomenon. In my opinion, Stuey is also bordering on this status and his exceptional statistics at Test level prove he is capable of anything. Both he and Shane have the skill and guile to take wickets on any surface against any batsman in world cricket, which is exactly what you need to win Test matches.

They both possess different trajectories and variations in flight, which is one reason why they can and should be successful together — even though people think two leggies can't work in tandem. Stuey is probably a bigger turner of the ball with both his leggie and wrong 'un, but Shane has many deadly well-disguised deliveries that strike the victim before he realises. In this vein, he is like a cobra lunging at its prey.

Stuey is what I'd call a big-match performer, who enjoys treading on the centre stage to showcase his talents and as such will always lift his game at Test level to produce his best cricket. He is stimulated by the pressure of the top-grade, likes to dominate and dictate terms to the batsman, and is willing to be taken for runs if the ultimate outcome is a wicket in his favour.

Some have said he is hot-blooded, which, of course, many of us are when we are passionate about what we do. To me such a trait is acceptable because it means you have pride in your performance. Knowing when you have crossed the line is the key.

We all have done things that we would like to change. Stuart has infringed in the past but that is exactly what that is ... the past. It is the present and future that count and people should be judged on now and not then.

He is a fine cricketer who likes his red wine, fine dining, novels and the hoick over midwicket. We should all be celebrating the fact that we have two outstanding leg-spinners in the same era, not trying to drive a wedge between them.

Stuey MacGill snares another victim in Sydney. The Australians congratulating him are (FROM LEFT) **Mark Waugh, Adam Gilchrist, Ricky Ponting and Shane Warne.**

January 5

Sydney

Australia v South Africa, Third Test Day Three, Sydney Cricket Ground

Australia 554 v South Africa 154 (62.2 overs: GD McGrath 3–35, SCG MacGill 3–51, SK Warne 3–47) and 2–209 (69 overs: G Kirsten 82 not out, HH Dippenaar 74)

Australia v South Africa, Third Test Day Four, Sydney Cricket Ground

Australia 554 and 0–54 (JL Langer 30 not out, ML Hayden 21 not out) defeated South Africa 154 and 452 (141.5 overs: G Kirsten 153, SM Pollock 61 not out; SK Warne 3–132, SCG MacGill 4–123) by 10 wickets

THE DAY STARTED WITH US being introduced to some of the firefighters who have worked so bravely over the past fortnight, and ended with another Test victory, a 3–0 clean sweep, this one by 10 wickets despite a South African fightback. It was an emotional victory, which confirmed our world No. 1 ranking, but though I knew that the past fortnight had been fantastic for the Australian squad, while we had been winning Test matches, the real heroes have been the firefighters saving lives and houses. That is why we decided to donate all our prizemoney to the bushfire relief fund. It's a small sacrifice for us, and we thought it was the right way to go. The ACB have matched us dollar for dollar, which means over 100 grand will be going to a very worthy cause. A handful of the firefighters escorted us for a part of our victory lap, featured in photographs and then shared a beer with the boys in the change-rooms, which they seemed to enjoy. And rightly so!

The South African comeback was spearheaded by Gary Kirsten, who made 153, and until he was dismissed we couldn't be sure of victory. Our two leggies bowled more than 87 overs between them, on a very flat deck, but their persistence and skill won the day for us in the end. It was appropriate that our two openers were there at the end, having blasted the required 54 runs in double quick time, as if they wanted to emphasise their dominance over the Proteas one last time. Their average partnership for the series was 114. Since they came together for the final Ashes Test of 2001, their average together is almost 118, including four double-century partnerships and one single-century stand.

Gary Kirsten (ABOVE) and Shaun Pollock (BELOW) were two South Africans who showed plenty of
fight during the visitors' second innings in Sydney.

I caused a bit of a storm at the post-Test media conference by saying that Haydos is currently 'playing as well as anybody's probably ever played the game'. Some people thought this was an outlandish statement, but he's in such complete control of his game, his balance is magnificent, his shot execution is first class, his temperament is really good and he knows his game really well, which all adds up to quite a package. And he dominates bowlers, which is not easy to do when you're opening the batting. When someone pushed me — did I really think Matty was better than Bradman? — I did have to retreat a fraction. 'I didn't see The Don play,' I replied, 'so … excluding The Don.' But Matty is still in amazing form, having hit a century in each of the three South African Tests.

The other major talking point was the fact that, despite the fact we'd completed a clean sweep, if we didn't *win* the upcoming Test series in South Africa, they would usurp us as the No. 1 ranked team in the world. A draw would be good enough for the South Africans to take over. It does seem that the International Cricket Council's computer that calculates the rankings needs some new batteries, but my attitude is that this isn't worth worrying about. Sure, we proudly held aloft the ICC's Test World Championship trophy when we did our victory lap, but if the series over there does end in a draw, after our 3–0 win here, it'll be pretty obvious who the No. 1 side is. All we can do is play hard and stick to our game plans; if we do that as well as we've done in the past three Tests then we'll be okay.

In any case, rankings don't make you play any differently or better. Our ambition is to more than maintain our current standards, to continue to lift the bar and to pull away from all the other teams. It's a tough ask, but opportunities to dominate your chosen profession are rare, so it's my job — with coach John Buchanan — to encourage this vision and help turn it into reality.

January 6

Sydney

THERE'S NOTHING MORE SATISFYING THAN a job well done, especially when the stakes are so high and the doomsday prophets have been predicting a

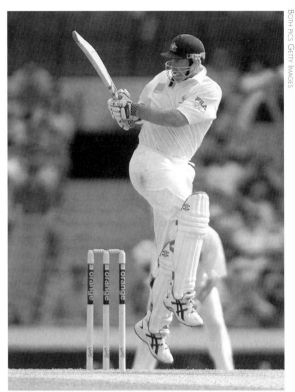

RIGHT: **Matthew Hayden hits the winning runs to compete a 3–0 sweep for the Australian part of our series with the South Africans.**
BELOW: **Gilly celebrates in Sydney, with the Aussie flag in his right hand and the ICC World Championship trophy in his left.**

fall from grace. Our 3–0 victory over South Africa in this Test series was a triumph for self-belief, hard work and dedication to the task at hand. Many critics had us as an ageing team, past our best and ready to be toppled as the No. 1 side.

Deep down, we believed we were still the best team in the world before the series against South Africa began, but with that title come high expectations and the knowledge that opponents always lift when playing the best.

It was interesting to note the build-up to the first Test in Adelaide, with a host of ex-South African players and supporters talking up their chances and dismissing ours as if we had assumed the mantle of Test cricket's top side through false pretences.

To be honest, after the first day's play in Adelaide I felt we had the South Africans' measure. On the opening day of a series, the nerves are usually heightened, emotions run high and clashes are inevitable. Not so on this occasion — our opponents were silent, seemingly in awe, even submissive. Buck had a different view from mine; he believed they were actually in control of their emotions and following a game plan. But my instincts told me that they were intimidated and quiet because they weren't confident about what lay ahead.

Our success and the impact it has had on many of our opponents has highlighted many of the advantages an experienced side can give you. First, players generally know their own games very well by their late 20s, as they have experienced both the ups and downs and know what works for them. They are generally more settled in their life away from cricket, with maturity and discipline being assets very helpful to seeing things in perspective. Years of accumulated knowledge are available for the benefit of the side, and Test matches take on an extra special significance as you know the end of your career is closer than the beginning. Every big match might very well be your last. The great thing about this 'ageing' Australian team is that we aren't satisfied with being successful; we also, more importantly, want to improve. When you think you can't get any better, then it is time for the younger brigade to come through.

Our next challenge is to win in South Africa, a task which we know will be tough as they are hurting and their pride has taken a beating. I'm sure they'll fight hard, but from our point of view we must win over there to stay No. 1.

That's all the motivation we need.

It's Just Like Playing in the Backyard

There was a period when neither Matthew Hayden nor Justin Langer was getting due credit for their talents. But there's something about them; maybe I saw something in them that others hadn't.

They're the sort of blokes who make everyone around them feel comfortable, because they're so strong, dedicated and focused, and I thought there was a big chance they'd come through if they were relaxed and confident. The people around them needed to believe in them, that was the key. I've always felt that if you create that kind of environment for all the members of the team — believe in them and back them all the time — that's a big start.

Today, they're established as Australia's opening batting partnership, with a record over the past 10 Tests that would be the envy of any pair in cricket's history.

They are cricket's version of 'Twins' — with Lang as Danny DeVito and Haydos as Arnold Schwarzenegger. The two of them look as if they're having the time of their lives and, what's more, they are. Consider this typical midwicket conversation …

HAYDEN: 'How good is this? It's just like playing in the backyard.'
LANGER: 'Have a look down at that crest and you know you're not.'
HAYDEN: 'That makes it even better!'

The opening batting combination is a team within a team — to be successful it must be united, resilient, combative, vigilant and proactive. To reach a level very few partnerships have managed over a lengthy passage of time, you must have that 'X' factor. And what is that? To me, it is all of the following: a genuine trust in each other, unflinching loyalty, mateship, knowing each other's game and personality, being able to sense the danger periods, enjoying each other's success, showing compassion, playing with pride and passion and working together to achieve a specific result. It's a mixture that very rarely comes together.

That is why Australian cricket is so lucky at the moment, for these two have a special bond, formed around friendship and belief, which appears to be indestructible.

Lang and Haydos are both strong, tough characters with a passion for life. Lang is a philosopher type, always searching for the meaning of life, gathering memories and images to inspire him to greater heights, not only as a sportsman but also as a person. A fiercely proud father of three, family is everything to him and talk of his three girls always animates and invigorates him.

Lang brings a well-rounded perspective to the side, as well as being a tangible example of a cricketer overcoming adversity to achieve his dreams and ambitions.

I'll never forget the answer he gave me to a question I put to him before his comeback Test at The Oval last August. I knew he was disappointed to be dropped (and he was unlucky, but someone had to be left out because Damien Martyn was in such commanding form that he had to be included), and I asked him how he was feeling. 'It feels like there are only two days to go until Christmas,' he replied with a grin. This pure love of the game certainly rubs off on his teammates.

Haydos is more of a dreamer, a lover of nature and all life has to offer. It's hard to find a moment when the boy from Kingaroy isn't loving life and laughing at something. He values friendship and loyalty, rather than any material possessions he could acquire. And he gives the team character and guidance as well as humour, often at your expense, particularly if Queensland have beaten NSW.

His love of nature is boundless. Earlier this season Matty stayed on the field during heavy rain in Hobart, because he just wanted to feel the rain, watch the clouds converge, hear the thunder and see the lightning. Everyone else scampered for cover, but Haydos was mesmerised by the awesome power of nature.

His best quote of recent times, and one he hates me referring to, came during last year's tour of India, when he was 12th man for a one-day game at Indore. Without thinking, he said, 'Geez, we've still got a pretty good batting line-up.'

One thing they both love is watching the sunset. At the moment, they're enjoying their time in the sun.

PART 2

THE VB SERIES
FROM TOP TO BOTTOM

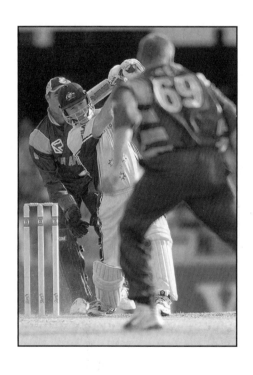

The master batsman of one-day cricket, Michael Bevan, during our opening match of the 2002 VB Series.

January 11

Melbourne

**Australia v New Zealand, VB Series,
Melbourne Cricket Ground, January 11**

New Zealand 8–199 (50 overs: CZ Harris 63 not out, DL Vettori 30; B Lee 3–43) defeated
Australia 176 (42 overs: RT Ponting 45; SE Bond 3–53, CL Cairns 3–42) by 23 runs

THIS WAS HARDLY THE START to the VB Series that we wanted. Not only did we lose — to a New Zealand team who appeared more focused and more determined than we were — but once again the blight of poor crowd behaviour reared its very ugly head to spoil what should have been a day/night of good clean entertainment for everyone, young and old, who attended the match. Two hundred and fifty people were thrown out of the MCG, and the match was delayed at one point during our innings after objects, including a bottle, were thrown at the Kiwi fieldsmen.

These disturbances are disappointing, because they stop the momentum of the game, and cruel, because the majority of the spectators are there to watch the game. It must take away from the spectacle and, quite frankly, it ruins one-day cricket from a player's perspective. When you have an opposing captain saying, 'All I worry about is the safety of my players', then I think that's a real black mark on Australian cricket crowds. After the game, I heard ACB CEO James Sutherland say, 'What concerns us is we've seen it all before. The behaviour of a small minority is putting the future of one-day cricket at this ground at risk.'

It's come to that.

This was a match we basically threw away. Having reduced New Zealand to 7–94, we were disappointed that they managed to get to 8–199, but it must be said that Chris Harris batted extremely intelligently and Daniel Vettori offered solid support. Two hundred was hardly an imposing target, but we batted very poorly, making too many basic errors. To need only 65 from the last 22 overs with six wickets in hand, and not get them; as I said, this was a game we should never have lost.

Perhaps we already believed the match was won, but as we are continually reminded in sport, complacency is a sure recipe for disaster. A mixture of lazy shots, poor communication and lack of match awareness had us in a state of disbelief as we contemplated out defeat in the change-rooms. My words to the team were brief and succinct: 'That was a poor performance, but let's move on and learn from our mistakes for the next match. This one's over now!'

January 14

Sydney

Australia v South Africa, VB Series,
Melbourne Cricket Ground, January 13

Australia 198 (48.5 overs: RT Ponting 51, SR Waugh 62; SM Pollock 3–25, JH Kallis 3–30) lost to South Africa 6–199 (48.3 overs: JN Rhodes 43 not out) by four wickets

THERE'S NO DENYING THAT OUR start to this year's VB Series hasn't gone to plan, but it is far from being the disastrous, desperate situation that many have suggested it is. First up, against New Zealand, we batted badly, and then yesterday against South Africa, while we hardly played as well as we can, there wasn't too much separating the two teams.

Batting first, we thought 220 would be a competitive score, on a wicket that was a bit up and down, not too good for strokeplay. In the end we finished 22 runs short, primarily because we didn't respect our wickets enough and played too many loose shots. There were also a couple of run outs, but that doesn't concern me as much, because there are always going to be run outs in the one-day game, as batsmen try to create opportunities for runs and with world-class fielders such as Herschelle Gibbs and especially Jonty Rhodes lurking around.

Our bowling, defending that slightly inadequate target, was good, though the South Africans' tactic of waiting for our 'fifth bowler' proved critical (Andrew Symonds went for 41 from seven overs and Michael Bevan conceded 10 from two). This has led to some negative reports, with many people now blaming our 'rotation' policy for our 0–2 start, especially the fact that the replacement of Ian Harvey with Symmo left us less experienced in the bowling department. While conceding that Harvs has often been excellent in the final overs of one-day internationals, these critics are forgetting all the terrific things that Symmo has done for us in the past couple of years.

It's human nature: whenever you have a vision or venture down the road less travelled, there are going to be people who don't share your views — either because it is different and they like things to always stay the same, or the bigger picture is blurred by what's happening right in front of them.

Our policy of giving each and every player in our squad an opportunity has worked brilliantly over the past couple of years. It is no coincidence that during this golden run for the most part the now controversial 'rotation' policy wasn't an issue; in fact it was applauded by many. To further back this theory up, we actually played 28 consecutive matches with different teams, never replicating the same XI, and through this sequence achieved enormous success. The concept of changing teams for each match isn't a new one in sport; in fact you only have to look at just about the most successful soccer team in the world today, Manchester United, to see that they regularly rotate all their players, including the England captain David Beckham. They do this to give the squad added depth: more players know the requirements of playing at the highest level by gaining experience while at the same time giving the rested players a chance to physically and mentally recuperate.

From our perspective, the bigger picture is the World Cup in 12 months' time. This is not to say we are not concerned about games in this VB Series, because we are committed to winning in the present as well, but what we don't want to happen is to arrive in South Africa for the World Cup next year having used the same 12 players in all the matches leading up to it and then suddenly panic when two or three players either fall victim to illness, injury or have a loss of form. We want 15 to 20 players capable of performing at the highest level under the most intense pressure

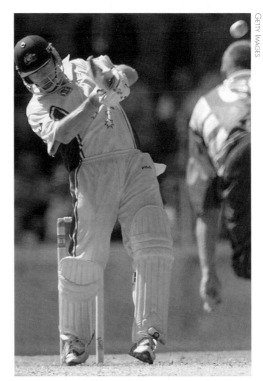

A pull shot during my 62 against South Africa at the MCG.

situations and the only way to do this is to have match experience under your belt. Make no mistake, the World Cup will be won by knowledge and experience, and we aim to have both these facets well and truly covered.

Getting back to our poor start in the two one-day games so far, it is easy to overanalyse and theorise when in truth the answer is simple. We lost both games through poor concentration, poor application and lack of match awareness. In both matches, we were in a position to either dominate or win the match but our consistency let us down. There were segments of each match in which we played disastrously and unfortunately they were at crucial times. The batting was often carefree and slipshod, with a lack of respect for the value of our wicket as well as for the quality of shots we played. This is an area that we have addressed and we all expect an improvement against the Black Caps in our next match. Bowling-wise, we have again had our moments but for some reason we have lacked the consistency to maintain the good work over the entire 50 overs. This must change and we also need to see a vibrancy and enthusiasm in the field, which will lift our intensity to the level required.

We lost momentum in each match and that cost us dearly. In limited-overs cricket, once a team has the ascendancy it generally keeps it — simply because the game is restricted to 50 overs per side. The game can fluctuate more often in the five-day Test matches, but in the one-dayers if you lose your way or throw away an advantage it is extremely difficult to pull things back. We've been giving ourselves too much to do, against two of the best teams in world cricket.

One must not forget that in this triangular series we have three out of the four semi-finalists from the last World Cup. The competition and skill level on offer is of the highest quality and therefore the occasional loss might almost be expected. From our point of view, we were a little under-prepared, having had no lead-up games coming into the tournament. There is a certain amount of adjusting from one form of the game to the other that needs to take place, and aspects of the mental side of cricket, such as knowing your game and the different strategies you need to employ to be successful, also have to be reassessed.

Six Tests in seven weeks was a big ask for the Australian Test team, especially as this run ended with the Sydney Test, where we spent 12 straight hours in the field. Consequently, I think it is fair to say that fatigue has played its part in our slow start. Most of the Test squad went straight into one-day action and didn't perform; perhaps we needed a couple more days to adjust to and be ready for the white ball.

It's now time to stand up and be counted, because it's been a long while since we lost three games straight. Realistically, it would be tough to make the finals from such a position. As the current World Cup holders, our reputation and status are at stake — the memory of holding that trophy, the pride we felt as we did so, will be just the inspiration we need to lift for the big games ahead. I just hope the selectors have patience and belief in the current squad and don't get drawn into the mountain of negative press we've had.

January 19

Brisbane

New Zealand v South Africa, VB Series, Bellerive Oval, Hobart, 15 January

South Africa 7–257 (50 overs: G Kirsten 97) defeated New Zealand 9–231 (50 overs: SP Fleming 85; AA Donald 3–40) by 26 runs

Australia v New Zealand, VB Series, Sydney Cricket Ground, January 17

New Zealand 9–235 (50 overs: CZ Harris 42 not out) defeated Australia 212 (47.2 overs: MG Bevan 66; CZ Harris 3–37) by 23 runs

New Zealand v South Africa, VB Series, The Gabba, Brisbane, January 19

South Africa 241 (48.3 overs: G Kirsten 43, JH Kallis 65, JN Rhodes 44, MV Boucher 51; SE Bond 4–37) lost to New Zealand 6–244 (49.1 overs: CL Cairns 102 not out) by four wickets

THE BIGGEST PLUS TO PAY-TV for a sports fan such as myself is that it provides an opportunity to watch important games from around the globe. Tonight, as I sat in my hotel room, I was able to grab the remote control and quickly become a keen observer of the India versus England match at the Lord's of the subcontinent, Eden Gardens in Kolkata. What a great spectacle! One hundred thousand people packed into the ground to see an excellent game of one-day cricket.

This was a real team effort by India, with many players contributing towards a 22-run victory, including some relatively inexperienced players, which augurs well for the future. The highlight of the match, though, was undoubtedly Marcus Trescothick's blazing 121, from 109 balls, which got England into a winning position until he was unluckily dismissed. This series is very important for England, who have only beaten Zimbabwe in recent times and need some tough wins to gather momentum and confidence for the times ahead, which include, of course, an Ashes series in Australia in 2002–03 and then the 2003 World Cup.

Australia, of course, also have some tough times ahead, starting tomorrow when we begin our quest to get back in contention for a finals berth in the VB Series and to return to the standard of play we prefer and one that the Australian public rightly demands.

The media criticism of the Aussie one-day team — which started as a whisper after we lost our opening game and has become something of an inferno now that we've started this VB Series '0–and–3' — continues on.

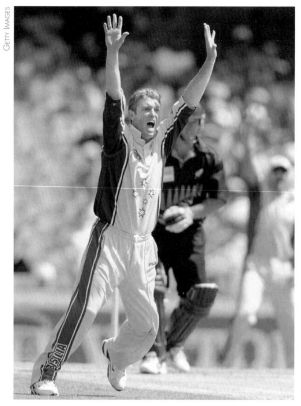

Ian Harvey in Sydney, appealing for lbw against the Black Caps' Lou Vincent.

Ryan Campbell — in the side replacing Adam Gilchrist, who had gone back to Perth to have a few days with his wife and just-born son — stumps Mark Richardson at the SCG.

The latest man to join the campaign is the former Test batsman-turned-radio commentator David Hookes, who has apparently labelled me 'the weakest link in Australia's one-day team'.

Of course, everyone is entitled to his or her opinion, but I have found it intriguing the way some former players who are now in the media seem so ready to put the boot in. I guess that's what they're now paid to do. I've found the last week has been very negative all round; if you read the papers you wouldn't think we are good enough to play cricket at all. Fortunately, I know what I'm capable of and I don't think my form is that bad. Indeed, I think I'm hitting the ball better than I was during the Tests.

All I can do is keep backing myself to do well and backing the side to start winning. There's no denying, however, that we're in trouble. History shows that it's extremely difficult to fight back to make the finals of this competition if you begin with three straight losses. And we haven't lost three straight since 1997–98. Despite this, I'm tipping a turnaround, starting with tomorrow's match against South Africa.

January 21

Sydney

**Australia v South Africa, VB Series, The Gabba,
Brisbane, January 20**

Australia 4–241 (50 overs: RT Ponting 80, DR Martyn 104 not out) defeated South Africa
214 (48.4 overs: ND McKenzie 68; GD McGrath 4–30, A Symonds 3–48) by 27 runs

OUR VICTORY OVER THE South Africans at the Gabba yesterday, secured in
front of a record crowd full of loud, loyal Aussie fans, was a professional
effort, much closer to how we know we can play, and much better than how
we performed in games one, two and three. Stars of the show were Damien
Martyn (104 not out) and Ricky Ponting (80) with the bat, and Glenn
McGrath, Andrew Symonds and Andy Bichel with the ball. And though
Jason Gillespie went for 60 runs from his 10 overs, he had the character to
come back to get the two key wickets of Jacques Kallis and Neil McKenzie.

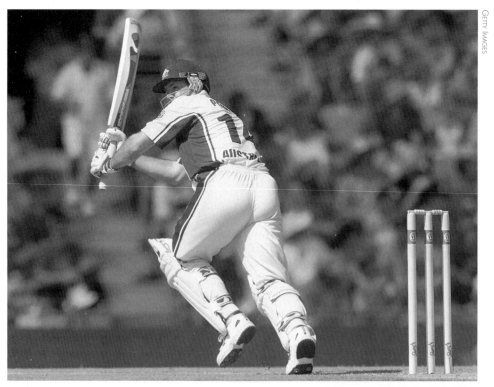

As he so often does, Ricky Ponting plays an important innings when his country really needs it.

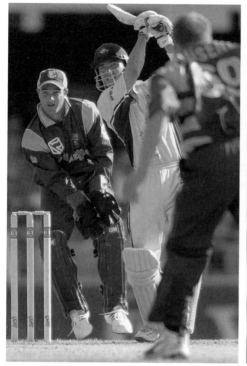

Damien Martyn puts Lance Klusener (back in Australia after his break during the Tests) over mid-off during his century at the Gabba.

Matthew Hayden has just caught Shaun Pollock, always a key wicket, and we are close to our first win of the VB Series.

Our fielding was excellent, too, and never better than when Symmo took a sensational catch off his own bowling to dismiss the dangerous Mark Boucher. All in all, an encouraging display, though we are very aware that owing to our poor start to the tournament, we cannot afford to relax, not even for a minute.

The great thing about winning is that everyone is happy — the players, selectors and supporters. It means you have played to your ability, followed your plans and fulfilled your potential.

The downside, of course, is that when you start to lose, particularly if you have set high standards beforehand, the criticism can be out of all proportion. Enormous expectations are often unrealistic and can be used against you to either increase TV ratings or to sell a few more papers with outrageous headlines and destructive comments.

We as a unit found this out during our three-match losing streak. Calls for wholesale changes have come from some critics, and our rotation policy has suddenly been the one and only reason for our demise. This system is one that has served us well in the recent past and one that has

Pressing Matters

Being the Australian captain invariably means that whenever you are near a cricket ground you are more than likely to be in demand for a press interview, photograph or a media conference. Unfortunately, these situations do not always go the way you'd like them to. Take, for example, an occasion earlier this season, just before the opening Test of the summer, when the NSW squad gathered at the Sydney Cricket Ground for training. The XII for the first Test had been chosen, but no announcement had yet been made as to who would be the 12th man.

I desperately wanted a solid net session in the lead-up to the Test, particularly as I had been laid up with the DVT problem for much of the previous six weeks. Before that, however, I obliged the gathered throng of journos with a 10-minute chat, during which I was asked whether or not Brett Lee would continue to be 'looked after' and start the Test, even though his form in the recent Ashes series had been relatively modest. Immediately, I was a bit aggrieved at the suggestion that I had been 'looking after' Brett in England, the implication being that I was unfairly favouring him over other members of the squad. Fair enough, he hadn't bowled at his best, but we had recognised that he is a renowned matchwinner and wicket-taker, characteristics in bowlers that are crucial to Test-match success.

Brett Lee celebrates dismissing Lou Vincent early in our VB Series opener in Melbourne.

Once I had gathered my thoughts, I replied, 'The 12th man at this stage hasn't been picked, so Brett — like everyone else — is vying for a place in the final XI. The only one certain to play at this stage is me, because I've been picked as captain of the team.' The selectors were hardly likely to name me as skipper and then make me 12th man. Yet from this conservative, non-headline-grabbing response to a question came the following headline, which screamed across the back page of a major newspaper the next morning: 'WAUGH SAYS HE CAN'T BE DROPPED'.

To say I was cheesed off is a gross understatement. This was way out of line, not least because it went to the absolute opposite end of the spectrum in regard to our team culture. We pride ourselves on the fact that within the squad everyone is equal, that no one is bigger than the game or more important than anyone else.

Sadly, as far as the press coverage of the team went, this was just the beginning. Many more unfounded stories and inaccurate quotes have been published so far this season, and the most frustrating thing is that there is nothing you can do about it. It seems, as far as the relationship between the media and the players is concerned, that the goalposts have been moved, that the rules have changed.

The worst example of this to date has occurred over recent days. A supposed feud between Trevor Hohns, the chairman of selectors, and me is dominating storylines. This came about after it was reported that we had been involved in an argument in the middle of the SCG before an important one-dayer. What actually happened was what always happens before a one-day international: a selector is designated to talk to the captain about who might be 12th man and sometimes 13th man, and then to have a general chit-chat about how things are going, maybe even about longer-term plans, future tours and so on. On this occasion, the conversation between Trevor and myself was extremely amicable, if longer than usual, as we focused on the fact that our form has been hot and cold.

Clearly, the sight of our extended conversation caught the attention of one or two of the print boys, because it became a hot topic over the following few days, to the point that upon our arrival at Brisbane airport I was bombarded with questions about the 'feud'. Unfortunately, it didn't matter how I responded, as the story had already grown into a monster. The truth didn't count. I explained that there was no 'feud', said that the story was totally baseless, but the next day's back-page headline was pretty predictable, and kept the story bubbling along …

'WAUGH DENIES FEUD WITH HOHNS'.

Andrew Symonds is one of the finest fieldsmen I have ever seen, as this catch off his own bowling — to dismiss Mark Boucher — clearly demonstrates.

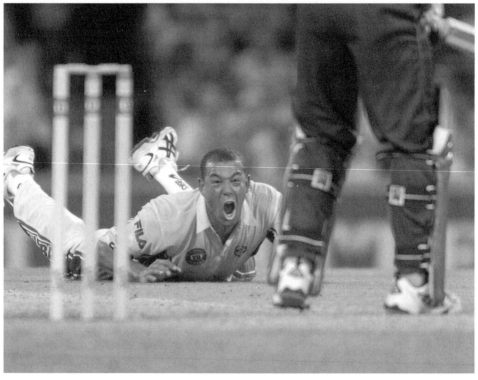

long-term benefits that sometimes may appear to some to conflict with short-term goals. Vision is needed and expected of leaders, but it will not always please or sit easily with others who don't want to or can't see the rationale behind an innovation. Change is difficult for people to embrace sometimes, because it can take them away from their comfort zone. Others might not understand the thought process behind new concepts. It is often easier in such situations to be negative, which is what many of our detractors are.

I know I'm starting to sound like a scratched record, but let me say one more time — the notion of giving opportunities to our whole squad has seen us win 18 and lose three in the calendar year 2001, which to me is an outstanding record for a one-day team. It has been used to help players rest and recuperate during the hectic and gruelling one-day schedules, thus allowing players to remain fresh and enthusiastic. It ensures we have a group of 15–20 players who all have international experience and can be called upon in the future to do a job with a degree of confidence. This is the crucial element to the plan, as Australia doesn't want to go into the World Cup and have an injury, illness or loss of form from one or more players and not have solid, dependable replacements we can rely upon. Only time will tell whether or not we are on the right track, but for now we will just have to cop the flak and stay strong in our beliefs.

One of my favourite sayings is, 'If you don't stand for something you'll fall for everything.' For me, that has never been more appropriate than now.

January 23

Sydney

**Australia v South Africa, VB Series,
Sydney Cricket Ground, January 22**
South Africa 106 (G Kirsten 44; GD McGrath 3–29, AJ Bichel 5–19) lost to
Australia 2–107 (18.4 overs: ME Waugh 55 not out) by eight wickets

IT'S AMAZING HOW QUICKLY THINGS can change. Two wins and we're right back in contention for a finals berth. And because we won last night's game so emphatically people are assuming that our campaign is back on track. The truth is that this game hasn't proved a lot, because our opponents were a long way from their best (and were without Jacques Kallis and Allan Donald), though I can't help but wonder whether this win will restore the psychological hold we have had over South Africa in recent times.

We swept to victory in just 19 overs this evening, with a 77-run partnership between Mark Waugh (55 not out) and Ricky Ponting (33) leading the way, and thus secured a bonus point that pushes us up to second place on the VB Series ladder. South Africa, however, do have a game in hand. Earlier, Andy Bichel had taken 5–19 — including a spell of 4–7 in 14 balls — as South Africa tumbled from 2–42 to 7–50 and eventually to 106 all out.

The bonus points concept is just one of a couple of innovations introduced for this competition. As well, the quick bowlers are now able to bowl one bouncer (going through no higher than head high) per over. Bonus points are earned in any VB Series match in which a team achieves a net run-rate in that match 1.25 runs higher than that of its opponent. Net run-rate is determined by dividing the run-rate you've achieved with the bat by the run-rate you've conceded with the ball.

Andy Bichel takes a blinder in Sydney to dismiss Makhaya Ntini and complete innings figures of 5–19.

Two West Australian century-makers in Sydney. RIGHT: Justin Langer celebrates another big hundred on the first day of the third Test against South Africa. BELOW: The following day Damien Martyn matched Lang's effort. Here he stylishly lofts a delivery over mid-off, with Mark Boucher's gloves indicating that the ball actually pitched on or maybe even just outside the leg stump.

ABOVE: **Boeta Dippenaar is clean bowled by Glenn McGrath late on day two of the third Test.**
BELOW: **Glenn** (CENTRE) **with man of the series Matt Hayden and Andy Bichel after we swept the home series.**

My opposing captains for the 2001–02 Australian season. RIGHT: Shaun Pollock appeals for the wicket of Mark Waugh in the January 20 one-dayer at the Gabba. BELOW: Stephen Fleming and I discuss what to do at the MCG after a small section of the crowd got rowdy during the opening encounter of the VB Series.

Three Australian quicks at practice during the Australian summer. LEFT: Glenn McGrath at the MCG nets. BELOW: Jason Gillespie working hard in Sydney as we seek to recover after a poor start to the VB Series.

LEFT: Brett Lee hams it up for the cameras during a stretching exercise with fitness co-ordinator Jock Campbell.

Michael Bevan at the MCG, keeping alive our VB Series hopes with an extraordinary innings.

LEFT: **Andy Bichel has just hit the winning runs against New Zealand on January 29, and Michael Bevan (102 not out) roars in delight.** BELOW: **The winning pair high-five as Bic's hit goes over the boundary rope.**

LEFT: **In the middle of an ordinary time for the Australian one-day team, this was a truly great comeback victory.**

RIGHT: **On the field, this was probably the low point of the summer. New Zealand's Daniel Vettori is elated, I'm crestfallen, as we crash to a dismal 77-run loss on Australia Day in Adelaide.**
BELOW: **Darren Lehmann came into the Australian team for the one-dayer in Perth and immediately made an impact with his skill and innovation.**

LEFT: **A heave over midwicket against the South Africans at the WACA.**
BELOW: **Brett Lee during his brief tornado of an innings that gave us real hope of getting a crucial bonus point from our final VB Series match.**

LEFT: **Unfortunately, we didn't do enough and missed the finals. Ten days later I was in Sydney, sitting next to Australian Cricket Board CEO James Sutherland as he told a media conference that I was no longer captain of the Australian one-day team.**

There were some suggestions that the SCG pitch was substandard, but I didn't agree. Sometimes it's good to have a pitch which gives bowlers a bit of assistance, because the usual thing for one-day cricket is a very flat wicket with a quick outfield and small boundaries. Had I won the toss today I would have done exactly what Shaun Pollock did: bat first. I'd go as far as to say it was an excellent cricket wicket — it wasn't a 106 pitch; something like 160 to 180 would have been a more realistic score to aim at.

X-ray Vision

After a one-day international in Sydney, the two captains and the man of the match are taken to a room underneath the Bradman Stand for a media conference. Last night both captains arrived for the conference at exactly the same time — something that rarely happens — and having won the match, I decided to let Shaun Pollock have his say first so he could head off home quickly. ACB Media Manager Brian Murgatroyd, man of the match Andy Bichel and I grabbed the only available seats, to one side of the 'head table' about 10 metres from the South Africa skipper.

Soon Shaun was asked about the health of fast bowler Steve Elworthy. Late in the South African innings, Elworthy had ducked into a Glenn McGrath delivery and was hit in the helmet. He batted on to make a plucky 18, but afterwards was taken to hospital for observation and a scan, which we'd learnt had cleared him of serious injury. 'Did the brain scan find any damage?' was the question put to Shaun, and as he began his answer I made the mistake of whispering to Brian Murgatroyd, 'I bet they didn't find anything.'

This was a reference to the fast-bowling fraternity's intelligence. Everyone knows this is a cricket joke with no credibility, but one the quicks have to put up with — just as we middle-order batsmen have to listen to the top order declaring that their job is to take the shine off the new ball to protect us. To my astonishment, a journo overheard me or read my lips, and by this morning I was being described as 'callous' and 'insensitive' as the 'incident' was written up in the papers. When I discovered the storm my remark had caused, I spoke with both Steve Elworthy and South African team manager Goolam Rajah, and to their credit they accepted my explanation and had no problems whatsoever.

January 28

Melbourne

Australia v New Zealand, VB Series, Adelaide Oval, January 26

New Zealand 5–242 (50 overs: NJ Astle 95, L Vincent 55, CL Cairns 39 not out) defeated Australia 165 (45.2 overs: MG Bevan 45; SE Bond 5–25) by 77 runs

New Zealand v South Africa, VB Series, Adelaide Oval, January 27

South Africa 5–253 (50 overs: HH Gibbs 89, JN Rhodes 55, MV Boucher 57 not out) defeated New Zealand 160 (45.2 overs: SP Fleming 43; N Boje 4–31) by 93 runs

THERE IS NO DOUBT THE low point of our season was our 77-run loss to New Zealand last Saturday night (Australia Day, January 26) in Adelaide, which has left our VB Series campaign in a perilous state. Not only did we lose, we conceded a bonus point. I would have to go back to the early stages of the 1999 World Cup to think of a less inspired effort by the Australian one-day team. It was a game where, rather than relishing the pressure, we succumbed to it. As a batting unit we got out every possible way we shouldn't have. It was like a nightmare, with players falling into traps we knew had been set. Once one wicket fell, the rest of us fell like dominoes. The only consolation I can see is that surely we can't play this badly again.

I'm really not sure what went wrong, other than the fact that we were outbatted, outbowled and outfielded. Shane Bond bowled magnificently to wreck our top order, after Nathan Astle, Lou Vincent and Chris Cairns batted extremely well. Afterwards, we had the Sunday off, and then — after a team meeting in which I was encouraged by the spirit and optimism of the lads — we had one of our best training sessions in quite a while, which promises a much better effort against the Kiwis at the MCG tomorrow night.

Once again, the press wanted to talk about selections, but I couldn't really help them. I'm not a selector, and the men who are have made it clear that in the short term at least the rotation policy has been jettisoned. I'll always believe it has considerable merit, for the reasons I've gone into, but for now I have no option but to deflect the press boys' questions on the issue.

Chris Cairns bounces Glenn McGrath during our dismal Australia Day in Adelaide.

One bloke who has come in for some criticism is the 'Freak', Ian Harvey, who has only played in two matches so far but could well come into the Australian team for tomorrow night. Harvs definitely has the ability to belong at the top level, he's just got to back his ability. There's no reason he shouldn't do well; his bowling has been excellent over the last 12 to 18 months and he's also done some good things with the bat. I keep thinking back to the series-deciding fifth match in India last April, when he and Bevo steered us to victory. He was superb that day and I'm sure he can reproduce that type of performance regularly if he believes he can.

I know we can turn our ordinary form around, and can assure you that the MCG crowd and the TV viewers will be seeing a side out there tomorrow that is desperate to win, but relaxed as well and confident in its ability. If we don't win tomorrow, it'll be because we're not good enough. And I can accept that as long as we go out there fighting and playing hard. Today we were weak and easily downtrodden — this was unacceptable and won't happen again.

January 30

Melbourne

Australia v New Zealand, VB Series,
Melbourne Cricket Ground, January 29

New Zealand 8–245 (50 overs: SP Fleming 50, CL Cairns 55, CZ Harris 41) lost to Australia 8–248 (49.3 overs: MG Bevan 102 not out; SE Bond 4–38) by two wickets

MY FIRST THOUGHT AFTER OUR remarkable victory against New Zealand last night in Melbourne was this: let's not waste one of the greatest ever one-day innings, played by Michael Bevan, by not winning our next match against South Africa, which we need to do to have any chance of qualifying for the finals. This victory, engineered by Bevo's genius, was a gutsy, courageous and rewarding win by a team that has been under siege during the past week. During this time we have never lost belief in what we could do, but have had to reassess and be honest with our performances, and be accountable for our actions. Before this game we committed to backing ourselves in every situation and to keeping things as simple as possible, by not overanalysing and complicating the game and, most importantly, by not playing to other people's expectations or comments.

Michael Bevan again showed why he is, in my opinion, the best batsman ever to have played one-day cricket. The 'Pyjama Picasso' created yet another masterpiece before our eyes. It was constructed gradually, executed precisely and delivered ruthlessly; in short, it was as good as it gets.

At 6–82, the outlook for us wasn't looking too rosy and my instructions were to make sure we at least got near the Kiwi total so that if we lost our run-rate would still give us an outside chance of making the finals. Deep down you always entertain thoughts of a miraculous win and we still had capable players in the shed, but realistically New Zealand had all but done the hard work needed for a victory. However, once the Warne/Bevan partnership became established, we had a base to launch an assault. And with 15 overs to go the boys decided they needed to make a move.

It was here that Bevo took charge, by picking off Chris Harris for three boundaries in an over to start the momentum and alter the tempo and mood of the game

The great skill of Bevo is his feel for the game, and for the right time to accelerate and also when to cut down his risks. He never likes to see the run-rate past about seven to seven and a half per over; if it's below this he knows he can win the match. By the time Brett Lee made his way to the crease we knew we had a chance to win, with all the lads sitting together in a tight bunch willing every ball to the boundary, second guessing where the boys were going to hit their next shots. Brett's innings was like Shane's — a tremendous supporting role that allowed Bevo to get us within

Black Caps quick Dion Nash has me caught behind in Melbourne, leaving us 5–65 and close to elimination from the 2002 competition.

Michael Bevan acknowledges the Aussie dressing-room after scoring one of the finest one-day hundreds I have ever seen.

striking distance. My nervous energy was spent reading *Shackleton's Way* between balls. One quote that hit me right between the eyes came from this book, a biography of one of the most famous of Antarctic explorers: 'Shackleton decided to take extreme risks when his options narrowed.' Bevo was living out these words, except for the fact that his actions were also controlled, which gave all the lads enormous belief.

As each over ticked by, the runs needed gradually caught up to the balls remaining. The mood was tense but exciting, as Bic made his way to the crease in a clutch situation, with all the lads transfixed on the action, except for Buck, who continued to meticulously record each ball in his notepad in writing so small only he could decipher the data. My only words to Bic before he went out to bat were, 'Don't hesitate, back yourself.' Simple, but the essence of one-day cricket.

Bevo's colossal hundred sent the room into a frenzy, as we clamoured to open the viewing window to show our appreciation of his feats. The game was ours now, but one more spanner was thrown into the equation when with six needed from seven balls, a crunching straight drive from the centurion, which was bound for at least two runs if not four, thudded into Bic's leg, stopping its path immediately and securing a dot ball for the Black Caps. The boys in the room threw their hands in the air, rocked on their chairs and cursed this cruel piece of fortune, before quickly settling back in to begin nominating Bic's next shot, from the first ball of the 50th over.

My gut instinct suggested a short ball, as Stephen Fleming positioned himself at slip in the hope of a fend from a Shane Bond throat ball. My tip was a boundary via a cut over the top of point. Others in the dressing-room thought a yorker might be the go, but in reality no one was too sure. Thankfully, Bic held his nerve and played two superb shots to get us home and set the change-room alight. It felt like a finals win and reminded me a lot of our Test victory against Pakistan in Hobart in late 1999, which in turn gave us a huge momentum in the following matches.

Buck recorded the events on his video camera and 10 years down the track we'll still be marvelling at Bevo's exceptional innings and our iron-willed belief that anything is possible. Walking out to greet Bevo on the field as he held his arms aloft acknowledging the crowd, Adam Gilchrist asked him how he felt. The reply, like his batting, was spot on and precise ...

'I feel like I am the man!'

Adam Gilchrist (CENTRE) **and Jason Gillespie are introduced to one of Melbourne Zoo's biggest attractions, as Travelex is announced as our sponsor for the upcoming tour of South Africa.**

Perth

New Zealand v South Africa, VB Series, WACA Ground, Perth, February 1

South Africa 5–270 (50 overs: JN Rhodes 107 not out, MV Boucher 58, SM Pollock 69 not out; DJ Nash 3–37) defeated New Zealand 8–203 (50 overs: CD McMillan 46) by 67 runs

WE FACE THE DIFFICULT ASSIGNMENT of needing to gain a bonus point in the final qualifying match against South Africa tomorrow at the WACA Ground if we want to make the finals. South Africa won a place in the finals last night by gaining a bonus point in what turned out to be a controversial 67-run victory over New Zealand. Because of a flaw in the bonus points system, the New Zealanders decided, once their target of 271 runs became an unrealistic possibility, to shut up shop and instead make sure they totalled less then 217 because that would enhance their chances of making the finals.

Why did they do this? The first relevant tiebreaker if teams are tied on the final qualifying table is head-to-head clashes, and in our four matches against the Kiwis, we've won one and lost three. So if we finish level with them on the final table, they will go through. If all three teams finish level, it'll come down to run-rates, and we have the better run-rate than New Zealand. Going into the match against South Africa, New Zealand had 17 points (four wins and a bonus point), South Africa had 13 points (three wins and a bonus point), and we had 13 points. By giving South Africa the bonus point, it puts South Africa on 18 points and means that if we beat South Africa without earning a bonus point in the final qualifying match tomorrow, we'll finish on 17 points, level with New Zealand and one behind South Africa. Which means we'd be out. If we beat South Africa and in the process earn a bonus point then New Zealand would be out.

I know Stephen Fleming was critical of the system last night, saying he was basically forced into asking his team not to play for a win, but I don't think — even after what happened last night — that we should be too quick to cast aside a system that is designed to try to reward adventurous play. It has worked well in domestic cricket and, when you think about it, it has added some interest to the VB Series. Rather than complain about it, we just have to play the cards we have been dealt.

Elsewhere, some sections of the media have made a fair bit of my reluctance to comment on selections and the future make-up of the side. My reticence is the result of the simple fact that it is not my job to comment on selections — that is the domain of the selectors. Yes, I have commented on selections in the past, but I have found this season that such openness can only cause me grief, generating headlines that neither I nor the team needs. And sometimes you want to keep the team to yourself, simply because you don't want to give your opponent a head start.

The inability of sections of the media to accept this has increased my general frustration with them, especially after some insinuated I was being malicious at the pre-match conference today. It pains me that when I give the team out early we are branded arrogant and if I hold onto it we are labelled as having a siege mentality. I explained that we wanted to keep the team to ourselves because we didn't want to help the South Africans in any way. But one or two representatives of local papers tried every different way they could think of to try to pry the information from me, as if my only motivation was to make their job difficult. It has been a long summer for everyone — players and the media — and maybe this exchange just reflected that.

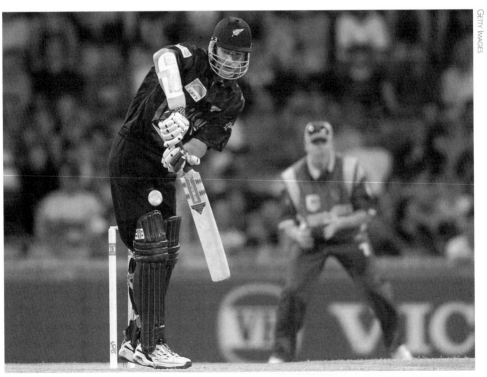

Daniel Vettori plays out time during the Black Caps' much-debated 'loss' to South Africa at the WACA.

February 4

Perth

Australia v South Africa, VB Series, WACA Ground, Perth, February 3

Australia 7–283 (SR Waugh 42, DS Lehmann 49 not out, B Lee 51 not out) defeated
South Africa 5–250 (50 overs: JH Kallis 104 not out) by 33 runs

DARREN LEHMANN, BACK IN THE Australian team after an extended absence, played extremely well yesterday with both bat and ball, but — besides the fact that we're out of the finals — the major talking point at the WACA was Brett Lee's extraordinary cameo at the end of our innings. Obviously, we needed to score as many as possible, and when Bing came in at 7–195 in the 40th over we were looking at somewhere between 240 and 260. Instead Bing went crazy at the end, hitting Allan Donald for a succession of sixes over long-off and we finished at 7–283. Bing top-scored with 51 from 36 balls. It meant we had to dismiss South Africa for less than 227 to secure the crucial bonus point, but the pitch was a beauty, Jacques Kallis was superb, and we didn't quite make it. They went past that magic target with 16 balls to spare, and got some cheap runs at the end to finish their 50 overs at 5–250.

Of course, I couldn't let the night go without getting myself into another sticky situation, after I muttered the immortal words, 'They're a bunch of cockheads', to our stand-in media liaison officer Pat O'Beirne as I walked away from the post-match media conference. It was not intended for anyone else's ears, but a young scribe from AAP picked up my comment and immediately wired it around the nation. As soon as this occurred every other journo had to run with the story as well, even if some of them didn't think there was much to it and put it down to a bit of steam being let off. I shouldn't have said it, and I wish I hadn't said it, but the conference was another ordinary experience, poorly handled by the local officials, and featuring a couple of local journos who kept persisting with one line of questioning long after it was clear I had answered their enquiries as best I could.

The exchange between me and the press began with me being asked about the South African game just gone …

Steve Waugh: We did our best, we played pretty well and we weren't quite good enough to get a bonus point, but I thought it was one of our best efforts of the one-day series. So from that point of view it was pleasing, but the overall missing out on the finals, we're disappointed. But we gave it our best shot today.

Question: Steve, when you batted first, how many runs did you think you needed to total to have a really good chance of getting that bonus point?

Steve Waugh: Well, 250 plus was what we were looking for. If we got 250, they needed 200, which was probably borderline so 280 was a good total and we thought that might be enough. But the wicket played pretty well.

Question: Steve, are there fears now of some reprisals and ramifications for not making the finals? The talk all along was World Cup preparation …

Steve Waugh: I don't think a lot's changed. We said we didn't play well in the first three games. From there we've won 4 out of 5, so I thought we played well at the end of the series. You've got to keep looking at the bigger picture. We've missed out on the finals here, but our last couple of games were pretty good, particularly today. South Africa are entitled, probably, to be joint favourites for the next World Cup and we beat them three times out of four pretty convincingly, so we've had some good results and some poor ones along the way. But you're not going to win every one-day game you play these days. Sides are pretty close. They study each other quite a bit and it's never easy to win one-day cricket.

Question: What sort of concessions do you make if there will be calls for changes?

Steve Waugh: Oh, well, if there's call for changes, there's call for changes. I mean, that's the selectors' prerogative. That's why they've got the job. If they want to make changes that they think can improve the side, then that's what they've got to do.

Question: Do you support that? Do you think changes should be made as captain?

Steve Waugh: I'm not a selector any more.

Jacques Kallis bats us out of the VB Series finals.

QUESTION: But as captain, you're going to be the one-day captain as well as the Test captain. Do you support changes to the one-day team for the World Cup build-up?

STEVE WAUGH: I'm not a selector any more.

QUESTION: What about as captain?

STEVE WAUGH: No, it doesn't matter.

QUESTION: Don't you have a say?

STEVE WAUGH: I have a say, but I don't pick the side.

QUESTION: If you had a say, what sort of things would you talk about?

STEVE WAUGH: I don't have a say.

QUESTION: Do you feel for your own position at all? I mean …

STEVE WAUGH: Look, everyone's under scrutiny, yes. You've got to perform. I don't expect any favours. If I'm not doing the job and someone's better, then they get an opportunity, but my one-day form wasn't too bad this series. It could have done with a big score, but consistency was okay. But as I say, leave it to the selectors to pick the side.

QUESTION: Can you see a need for fresh legs in the field in any way … some young players, young legs in the side?

STEVE WAUGH: Well there's always that option, but as I say, we finished off pretty well and if you look at the last 12 months, our one-day record is pretty good — we've won about 70 per cent or 80 per cent of games. I don't think any other side in the world has done that, possibly with the exception of South Africa. So you can make quick changes if you want, but I think you've got to make sure that if you're going to make changes — are they better players or are you improving the side?

QUESTION: You've had some tough series back to back. Do you think a week off might be a bit of a blessing in disguise before you leave?

STEVE WAUGH: I don't think it's a week off. I think we're back playing for the states now, so there's a couple of days off, but I don't think it's a lot of time off. And we'd rather be, obviously, in Melbourne and Sydney, but it's not to be. And yeah, we've just got to get ready for the South African series now.

QUESTION: Steve, there's been a bit of a tendency, especially this season, for Australian players not to play for their states. Do you think it would be opportune for players all to go back?

STEVE WAUGH: Well for the players who haven't played state cricket it has been a judgment by the support staff and the medical staff. It's not as if blokes are not playing because they don't want to. There's a reason why they're not playing and once again they will be assessed before the next matches, but I think quite a few of the guys will play the next one-dayers for their states.

QUESTION: Jason Gillespie didn't play today. Is there an injury concern?

STEVE WAUGH: Not that I know of, no. Unless you've picked one up.

QUESTION: I thought he might have been injured, or else why didn't he play? I think he should have been in the starting XI.

STEVE WAUGH: You're not a selector.

QUESTION: Did you think he had something to add today? Could he have made a difference?

STEVE WAUGH: Guys, we just won the game by 30-odd runs, you know. We can't have everyone in the side. We've got 13 players. Two guys have got to miss out.

QUESTION: Steve. Darren Lehmann obviously had an exceptionally good game.

STEVE WAUGH: Yeah.

QUESTION: Now I know you don't have any selection say, but nonetheless would you have welcomed him in the team several games earlier and might that have made an important difference?

STEVE WAUGH: We're talking about hindsight here. I mean, if you suggested that three games ago then it might be a good point but suggesting it now ...

QUESTION: (inaudible)

STEVE WAUGH: Were they? Were you one of them?

QUESTION: Yes.

STEVE WAUGH: Well maybe we should have listened to you.

QUESTION: Is it possible for you to answer the question?
STEVE WAUGH: I just did.

QUESTION: Steve, the opening combination was in conjecture and has been changed a bit during the course of the series. You showed faith in the traditional pairing. Was that your choice? Is that your preferred option? Do you want them to be the opening combination?
STEVE WAUGH: Well I've got a lot of faith in those guys. Yeah, I think they've done very well over a long period of time and yeah, I've got faith in all the players. That's why — we lose a couple of games, people want to make a lot of changes, but you've got to have faith in the players. We finished off the series pretty well. Darren Lehmann had a good game today, but you know you don't want to change a side too much. We've done very well over the last couple of years. You lose a couple of games and everyone wants to be an expert, everyone wants to change the side. You've got to have faith in your players.

QUESTION: Do you see yourself increasing your workload as a bowler?
STEVE WAUGH: Not a great deal. I think there's better options than me, bowling-wise. But if I can get a few overs in, it helps the balance of the side, then I'll try and do it. Today, it didn't quite work out, I guess. We had to really mix and match for the fifth bowler. Darren did pretty well, but realistically two of our frontline bowlers went for over 50 runs, so it wasn't really the fifth bowler that was a problem today. But it would be nice to bowl a few overs occasionally.

QUESTION: Why aren't Ricky and Damien Martyn being used as back-up bowlers?
STEVE WAUGH: Well, you can't use everyone. I mean you've got to make a choice as a captain and that's my job out there. I do it to the best of my ability. Michael Bevan bowled a couple today, Darren Lehmann bowled a few overs. You know, you can't bowl everyone. You've got five front-line bowlers generally and they are the guys that are picked to do the job.

QUESTION: Who do you fancy to win the finals?
STEVE WAUGH: I think it will be a close final series. Both teams are capable of beating each other. South Africa the last couple of years

Late in the day during our match against South Africa at the WACA, as it becomes clear that we won't be playing in this season's one-day finals.

have been a very good one-day side. New Zealand have played well this series. But, as for the win, I'm not really sure.

QUESTION: Steve, can I just revisit the bonus point system that yesterday you didn't seem to want to talk about. It's the end of the series now. What do you think of the bonus point system that's been talked about.

STEVE WAUGH: I think it's up for review. See how it goes. At the start of the series it seemed like a very good idea. At the end of the series you've got to assess how it affected the last couple of games and whether that's good for cricket or whether it's not good for cricket. So, I'm not really part of that review process, but I think they need to have a good look at it.

QUESTION: Have you got concerns about it?

STEVE WAUGH: I think everyone that watched the games would have some concerns. But we knew what the system was before the series started so there's no complaints from us.

QUESTION: Did you realise pretty early today that South Africa set a target of 227 to stop you getting in?

STEVE WAUGH: Yeah, well, that was always going to be the case. I mean they probably didn't want to play us in the finals. We've done well against them this year and 227 was still a fair-sized target.

QUESTION: Will you raise it at the next captain's meeting?

STEVE WAUGH: I don't know when the next captain's meeting is. But if it is on the agenda I will certainly talk about it, yeah …

And that was the end of the press conference. One of the journos thanked me for coming down, and I said what I shouldn't have said. When Board CEO James Sutherland was asked this morning to comment, he replied, 'A couple of ACB representatives were there, I have spoken to them, and it would appear it was a pretty difficult press conference at the end of a difficult match and a long summer. Waugh made an off-the-cuff remark to an ACB person on the way out. I understand the context of that, I have spoken to Steve Waugh and I won't be taking the matter any further.'

February 9

Sydney

New Zealand v South Africa, VB Series First Final, Melbourne Cricket Ground, February 6

New Zealand 190 (47.5 overs: SP Fleming 50, CD McMillan 73; M Ntini 5–31) lost to South Africa 2–191 (45.1 overs: JH Kallis 59 not out, HH Dippenaar 79 not out) by eight wickets

New Zealand v South Africa, VB Series Second Final, Sydney Cricket Ground, February 8

New Zealand 175 (41.1 overs: L Vincent 43, CL Cairns 57; AA Donald 3–29, JH Kallis 3–23) lost to South Africa 4–173 (38.1 overs: HH Gibbs 46, JN Rhodes 61 not out) by six wickets (D/L method). South Africa wins best-of-three finals series 2–0.

A LOT HAS BEEN SAID about the rights and wrongs of the bonus points system that ended up separating the three teams on the final ladder for the VB Series, but much of it ignores one simple reason behind our early exit from the tournament. We were slow out of the blocks and we paid for it.

As I've said before, with the short time lag between the end of the Test series and the start of the VB Series, there was no chance for a lead-up game, as our opponents enjoyed, and without such a rehearsal we lacked the sharpness required at the top level in our first three matches. That lack of sharpness was exploited by two excellent one-day sides and, mixed in with some poor shot selection in those games, we found ourselves under the pump.

I guess bonus points played a part in our elimination, but if we had won even one of those three early matches it would not have been an issue. As for whether bonus points are the right way to go, that is ultimately up to the International Cricket Council to decide. Having thought about it a bit more, in my view there is a case for reviewing the system in the light of what has happened in this tournament, but I'm not sure it's the major issue some people are trying to turn it into. After all, a couple of weeks ago everyone was saying what a brilliant idea they are and they certainly helped contribute to the excitement that was a feature of this closely fought series.

One simple solution may be to make net run-rate rather than the head-to-head records of teams that finish level on points the first tie-breaker in

Allan Donald ends his final tour of Australia with the VB Series trophy.

deciding who finished above whom. On that basis, there could be no repeat of New Zealand's defensive effort at the end of their match against South Africa in the competition's penultimate qualifying game, as by blocking out they would have been hurting their own net run-rate rather than exploiting the system to help their cause.

All the same, hindsight is a marvellous thing. The fact remains we missed out on the finals series and it hurts like hell. It's now up to us to learn lessons from defeat and the main one for me is that if you have the momentum in one-day cricket you must do all you can to keep it. Never take the foot off the pedal, even for a moment. In Tests, momentum can change and over the course of five days you have the chance to win it back, but in one-day games if you lose control you usually lose the game.

The hurt that I and the rest of the players felt at not being in the finals was massive. But rest assured, that failure has made us realise how much we enjoy being in the winner's circle. And that is a place that we want to return to as soon as possible, starting with our tour of South Africa that begins on February 14.

February 13

Sydney

IT'S NEVER EASY TO TELL someone they've been dropped — regardless of whether it is expected or comes as a complete shock. I know this from first-hand experience, as I've delivered the news many times to fellow players and can vouch for that nauseating feeling in the pit of one's stomach, the sweaty palms and the shallowness of breath that accompany the moment.

At around 3pm last Monday, two days back, the day of the Allan Border Medal night, selection chairman Trevor Hohns began a conversation in my room at the team hotel, discussing the make-up of the team for the first Test in South Africa and the line-up required for the first tour game. It was shortly after that we were to begin talking about the one-dayers.

Surrounded by the media as chairman of selectors Trevor Hohns (LEFT) and ACB CEO James Sutherland (CENTRE) announce that my time as Australia's one-day captain has come to an end.

After being told I'd been sacked, I quickly decided I wanted it all out in the open.

Suddenly a sentence came out of the chairman of selectors' mouth that hit me like a sledgehammer and hung in the air for what seemed like an eternity.

'We have decided to go in a different direction and you are not part of that plan.'

For a moment I hoped he had mixed up his words and it wasn't me he was talking about. But then reality set in. Much of the next five or so minutes remains a blur. I know I thought about never playing one-day cricket again and missing out on a World Cup campaign.

It was a strangely subdued time, with neither of us comfortable or animated. In fact, it felt as if we were rehearsing lines from a move script.

I had 20 minutes before we had to get together as a team, so I had a little time to reflect on the impact of the conversation just gone. Many things raced through my mind. I firstly wanted to call my family and give them the respect and courtesy of being the first to know. As has been the case many times in the past, my wife was able to put things into perspective by saying, 'Things happen for a reason. It mightn't be clear right now, but it will work out in the end.'

I followed this up with a call to my manager, who was both shocked and supportive. The moment I put down the phone down I vowed to see this as a setback; it was not to be a career-ending move but a career-enhancing one. No matter what the final outcome down the track, the spirit and will to begin the fight had just begun.

The fire from within is something hard to explain and only the owner knows how it works and when it is still burning. Many would say my time is up and suggest I should walk away. After all, I've had many years of playing for Australia and have so many great memories. But if I did this I would not be true to myself. Age is irrelevant. It is only a number and whether you are 18 or 80, numbers don't guarantee attitude, commitment and desire.

If I had any doubts about this, they were dispelled when I arrived home and started playing with my two-year-old son Austin. Standing on the floorboards with mini-bat in hand he mimicked a cricket stance then began banging his bat up and down, encouraging me to join in.

'Cricket, daddy ... throw me the ball.'

The empty seats at the SCG reflect the way I felt when first told I would no longer be leading the Australian one-day team.

Media commitments over, finally I can duck into a car and head for home.

With that I rolled the plastic ball along the ground and he smashed it past me, far enough to hit the toys swinging from a frame inches above baby daughter Lillian's head. Big Bird copped it in the back.

The joy on his face was obvious and uninhibited. It came from within and that's the way it has to be. That's what I have always felt.

The media conference where my sacking was announced was one I thought would be an ordeal, even though it was one that I had initiated to clear the air. I feared a leak before the team is officially announced and wanted it all out in the open. Both Trevor and James Sutherland had their say and I respected and appreciated their words, even though I could not agree with all of them.

It's strange but ever since I found out about my demotion, I've felt an inner strength come to the surface. In many ways that is due to the enormous support of the cricketing and general public, as well as family and friends who have been tremendous. I feel as if I owe them one more crack at the one-day game and that is what I am going to do …

Have a go.

PART 3

AUSSIES ON THE VELDT 2002

The 2001–02 Australians, the 10th Australian Test team to tour South Africa, photographed at the Wanderers Ground in Johannesburg. BACK ROW (FROM LEFT): **Errol Alcott (physiotherapist), Stuart MacGill, Darren Lehmann, Damien Martyn, Matthew Hayden, Jason Gillespie, Andy Bichel, Shane Watson, Brett Lee, Jock Campbell (fitness co-ordinator), Mike Walsh (cricket analyst).** FRONT ROW: **Justin Langer, Glenn McGrath, Adam Gilchrist, Steve Bernard (manager), Steve Waugh (captain), John Buchanan (coach), Mark Waugh, Ricky Ponting, Shane Warne.**

PREVIOUS AUSTRALIAN TEST TOURS OF SOUTH AFRICA

Season	Australian captain	South African captain	Tests	Won	Lost	Drawn
1902–03	J Darling	HM Taberer*	3	2	–	1
1921–22	HL Collins	HW Taylor	3	1	–	2
1935–36	VY Richardson	HF Wade	5	4	–	1
1949–50	AL Hassett	AD Nourse	5	4	–	1
1957–58	ID Craig	CB van Ryneveld**	5	3	–	2
1966–67	RB Simpson	PL van der Merwe	5	1	3	1
1969–70	WM Lawry	A Bacher	4	–	4	–
1993–94	AR Border	KC Wessels	3	1	1	1
1996–97	MA Taylor	WJ Cronje	3	2	1	–

* JH Anderson led South Africa in the second Test of the series, EA Halliwell in the third.
** DJ McGlew led South Africa in the first Test of the series.

February 14

Sydney to Potchefstroom via Johannesburg

I WOKE AT 6.30 THIS morning feeling extremely positive about what had happened yesterday and also about what lay ahead. This challenge I'm about to take on — essentially to sustain my career — will be one in which it seems I'll be obliged to constantly counter the pessimism of the doomsday merchants, and their accomplices, the 'safety in numbers' brigade, who are content to sit on the sidelines predicting negative outcomes. I don't want to be brought down by these people; rather, I will be sustained by positive, infectious personalities and people who have vision, desire and want to achieve something in their lives. Many individuals have given me strength over the past couple of days, including friends, former players, current teammates and family, so many good people from the cricketing and general public. My wife Lynette has been a

The first media conference as a Test captain in South Africa. To my left is the Gerald Majola, the Chief Executive of the United Cricket Board of South Africa.

Andy Bichel arrives in Johannesburg at the start of our five-week Test tour.

pillar of strength and wisdom, more so than she would ever realise, and has given me that little bit extra, the 'X' factor to keep going.

Being dropped as a one-day captain was always going to be big news, but even I was astounded at the reaction to, comment about, and analysis of the event. But having received such enormous support from the majority of people, I feel calm, relaxed and confident on this day of our departure to South Africa.

My two eldest kids, Austin and Rosalie, find it quite amusing that Dad's on the TV so often, sometimes — as it was this morning — even before The Teletubbies begin to run amok just after 7am. Rosie is a schoolgirl these days, fully aware of what I do and that the kids at school know who I am. Thankfully, she accepts it and even enjoys it when her dad is pointed at and talked about as 'Steve Waugh'. I've explained to her that I'm now captain of the 'white' team, but not of the 'yellow' team.

When I told Lynette the news the other day by phone, she shed a few tears, a reaction that didn't escape Rosie standing nearby. Now Rosie is very perceptive of moods and body language, and she could work out the gist of this emotional conversation. As Lynette tried to work out a way to explain what was happening, Rosie asked matter-of-factly, 'What's the matter Mummy, isn't Daddy captain anymore?' That's the great thing about kids, they're so innocent and unaffected and just say it how it is.

Of course, there was some last-minute packing to be done before the mad dash to the airport for the flight to South Africa, in between getting the kids their Weet-Bix for brekkie, but by the time the cab arrived I was almost ready. Fortunately, I'd been able to procure a replacement passport in three hours yesterday after the original document went missing. Kids can also be handy in passing the blame in such situations, and we decided that either Austin or Rosalie had misplaced the offending item, a conclusion that led to something akin to anarchy in the Waugh household for a good 30 minutes just prior to me setting off for one of the most important press conferences of my career. A few quick calls and some much-needed help by Jo at the ACB and Donna of NSWCA got me out of a tricky situation. Even so, I still had to rush to get two new passport photos taken before I could sit down in front of the cameras and reporters at the Sydney Cricket Ground.

Saying goodbye is always a gut-wrenching experience and with each new addition to the family the anguish is magnified. Looking back through the cab window and seeing Austin, Lillian, Rosalie and Lynette standing between and behind the wrought-iron gates was almost a surreal experience, as they waved their hands in the air. Being successful will be the compensation for the sacrifice.

Another press conference awaited me at the airport, as we launched the tour and introduced our tour sponsor, Travelex. Inevitably, the regulation questions about the tour and the sponsorship were quickly followed by further enquiries about the 'hot topic': my demotion. To be honest, answering these questions this time wasn't that hard, because the scribes had covered most things at yesterday's announcement. Then it was time for a quick chat with Steve Liebmann from Channel Nine's *Today* show, after which I checked in and met up with the boys.

The news of yesterday might have been the main subject outside the team, but we quickly became more concerned with another question: what was the correct tour tie? Some of the boys were wearing the red 'collectors' edition and others the co-ordinated tie of past tours. For Andy Bichel, this was a minor matter compared with the location of his passport.

A Tale of Two Conferences

My sacking as one-day captain is dominating the sports pages, and some of the front pages, too. Inevitably, it was the main talking point at two press conferences many hours and many kilometres apart, one in Sydney before we left Australia and another in Johannesburg after we landed in South Africa.

I tried to deflect the questions about the captaincy, on the basis that it had all been covered in the previous 24 hours. I can't imagine there is any question that has been left unasked, and told the press that the team would not be dwelling on the issue. 'It's been dealt with, it's over and it's time to move on,' I said at Sydney Airport. 'We've just got to get everyone in a positive frame of mind for that first Test.'

'I'm really positive about this tour,' I continued. 'I'm looking forward to playing Test matches and maintaining our status as the No. 1 Test side in the world. I've had a lot of good feedback from friends and family, and the public out there have been outstanding, so I feel pretty good.'

A couple of the reporters in Jo'burg seemed genuinely miffed that I would not be playing in the World Cup in South Africa in 2003. 'I haven't given up hope of being here next year,' I told them. 'I'm out of the side at the moment, but I plan on making the next World Cup, so I've got to score a lot of runs next year and force my way back into the squad.'

But back to this tour. Would the selection drama have a negative impact, had it happened at an ideal time as far as this tour was concerned? 'We've just got to get together,' I replied. 'They [the selectors] have hinted at more changes [to the one-day squad] before the Test match series begins, so we'll try to get those out of the way and get the guys concentrating on Test-match cricket. The answer to that is no, it's not an ideal time.'

Of course I should have added that there is never an ideal time for such a decision, given the magnitude of it and the crowded nature of modern cricket itineraries.

He'd left it at home when he flew down from Brisbane yesterday, but was lucky in that John Buchanan was travelling to Sydney this morning and thus had time to collect the missing item on his way to the airport. This was a sound Plan B, but once here Buck forgot to hand it over before he darted off on a shopping spree. Thankfully Brett Lee, who knew of Bic's plight, spotted big 'Pluto' and reminded the coach that he had a spare passport in his possession.

Waiting in the Qantas Club lounge gave me an opportunity to meet and chat one-on-one with the new boy, Shane Watson. He seems quietly confident and determined as he sets out on what I'm sure will be a great learning experience for him. Talking to him took me back to my international debut as a 20-year-old; I hope I can give him the support and guidance that he needs and desires.

As is usual, as soon as we boarded and put our carry bags in the overhead lockers, most of the guys changed into their civvies. Our primary motivation for this is to avoid crushing the team uniform, which needs to look fresh and as crinkle free as possible when we arrive at the other end, in this case some 14 hours away in Johannesburg. For Mark Waugh, this simple task became somewhat embarrassing when the flight attendant barged into the toilet as the kit was coming off. It was red faces for those involved amid a chorus of laughter from the rest of the lads.

Three movies, numerous in-flight meals, a novel and 14 hours later, we landed in Jo'burg. As always on long flights, I slept very little, whereas others, such as Warney and Brett Lee, remained welded to the pillow for the entire journey. Of course, even after we hit the tarmac the trip wasn't over, with an hour wait to get through customs while the security guards assigned to protect us through the scrum of fans and onlookers beyond the customs gates seemed more interested in getting the boys' signatures than apprehending any offenders. For Buck and myself, it was off to a press conference with minds in a coma and eyes irritated as if someone had thrown a handful of sand at them. Most questions were negotiated with comfort, considering I'd had them all plus more in the past couple of days. Unusually, John had to answer a few questions — normally the media tend to ignore him, preferring to focus on the players, to the point that he often seems like a cardboard cutout tacked on the end. Here, Brisbane Broncos master coach Wayne Bennett would have approved of Buck's discipline, and the shortness and scarcity of information our coach divulged.

Finally, it was time to make our way onto the bus for the next leg of the trip, a drive to Potchefstroom, located south-west of Jo'burg. Not surprisingly, the two-hour journey was a very subdued and quiet affair.

Despite my weariness, the nine-hour time difference confused the body clock enough for me to wake up at 12.52am, just three hours after I hit the sack. Not even the fact that I'd brought my own pillow from home could help me. But a couple of sleeping tablets sent me off with the fairies from 1.30am to 4.30am, and then I caught up with the curling at the Winter Olympics — which acted as a better sleeping tablet than the yellow footy bombs I'd taken earlier. I finally woke at 7.50am satisfied with my accumulated shut-eye.

February 15

Potchefstroom

THIS MORNING WAS SPENT TRACKING down various gadgets, such as adaptors and internet connections, to make life in a hotel room somewhat normal. After that, Jock Campbell had us all in the gym by mid morning to flush any jet lag out of our systems and get us going, which was particularly important given that our first game is only two days away. Some mirth was generated in the swimming pool, when the lads were forced to don swimming caps that for many appeared to be a tad tight. Magilla's, especially, had to be wrestled on.

The rehabilitation process continued into the afternoon, with half an hour of physio and a 30-minute rub-down from our new team masseur, Lucy, who has joined us from Perth. The obligatory function really made us feel as if we were on tour, but it was a short, painless ceremony where team manager Steve Bernard stole the show with a speech that somehow linked the mayor's wife and daughter to us receiving the keys to the city, which had been presented to us earlier at the gathering. Continuing on my challenging week, I had missed the team bus to the function by 10 seconds and had to be picked up later. While it was my fault in being tardy, I felt a little aggrieved that the 'ger hadn't added up the numbers correctly to realise that the captain wasn't on board. At least I won't make the same mistake again.

Our coach John Buchanan in close-up, at Jo'burg airport soon after our touchdown in South Africa.

February 16

Potchefstroom

A 4.52AM AWAKENING SIGNALLED THAT the body clock had begun adjusting to the time difference. At least it was a convenient time to call back home and speak to the family.

Today was designated as the time when the team would oblige all the local media by answering their questions. Not surprisingly, I was repeatedly asked about the one-day situation; this has now become like a 'groundhog day' press conference. The positive today was the appointment of Ricky Ponting as the new one-day captain, which was relayed to me at 10.15am by the CEO of the Australian Cricket Board James Sutherland. Punter is an excellent choice, a man who has the respect of the players and who wants the job. He has an inquiring mind, is fiercely competitive and is improving with age, which — when it's all added up — totals a complete package. What he hasn't handled yet, or

Ricky Ponting meets the media soon after it was announced that he would be the next captain of the Australian one-day team.

knows about, is the extra demands and burdens that the captaincy brings. Issues both on and off the field will now fall under his umbrella and he will become public property, but this is a challenge that awaits him and one I'm sure he'll embrace. For Gilly and Warney, the decision to promote Ricky would have been a tough call, as I know they both had aspirations to the position. I called all three after I found out about the Board's verdict, but then couldn't get back to sleep, so I continued on with *Shackleton's Way*.

Today's training was reasonably solid, but the lads are still very tired from the journey and the intensity wasn't at its usual level. Still, the guys' attitude was commendable. Here, well above sea level, it is tough work for the quick bowlers to get their breath and stamina, and we all must adapt as quickly as possible as the first Test is less than a week away. Bearing this in mind, our choice of dinner at a seafood restaurant loomed as a major gamble, even though it came highly recommended. Thankfully our mail was spot on and the feed was 'top shelf'.

February 17

Potchefstroom

South Africa A v Australians,
North West Cricket Stadium, Potchefstroom
Australians 3–218 (60 overs; RT Ponting 93 not out, ME Waugh 62,
SR Waugh 18 not out)

ONCE AGAIN THE BODY CLOCK switched on at around 5am, which isn't ideal, especially on a match day. Nowadays, I struggle to go back to sleep once the eyes open, perhaps a legacy of having three young children at home.

No one was more pleased to win the toss than our trio of quicks, who cheered loudly, knowing full well I'd bat if the coin fell my way. Even though the wicket looked underprepared, I wanted us to try to have two innings with the bat so everyone would have an opportunity to gain confidence and form leading into the Test. Matthew Hayden and Justin Langer again did a tremendous job at the top of the order, safely negotiating a very difficult first hour against a testing new ball attack. From this solid platform, Ricky Ponting and Mark Waugh played with authority until Mark fell after looking set for a 100. My 18 not out felt fantastic, almost as if I clicked into gear for the first time in a while. It can be a fine line between feeling settled and feeling fidgety, and today I felt in the groove — a very encouraging sign for the tour ahead.

Back at the hotel I checked on the internet to catch up on all the news from back home and to keep in touch with all things Oz. Unfortunately for Michael Slater, he made the headlines for an incident in Sydney grade cricket when he was felled by a young Australian under-19 fast bowler. With blood streaming down his face, Slats apparently clashed with a photographer on his way off the field, which was then given great prominence by the media outlets. Of course, I don't know all the details of this incident, but even so I couldn't help thinking how sad it is to see how the reporting of sport has changed of late, with no leeway or compassion given in any circumstances. In this case, it appeared that no consideration was given to the fact that Slats had just been hurt. Instead, these days it seems anything goes, regardless of the damage it causes, so long as an extra one or two papers might be sold.

While our batting order began the tour in fine style, **Brett Lee** (CENTRE, SIGNING AN AUTOGRAPH) **and Jason Gillespie** (FAR RIGHT) **took time to introduce themselves to the locals.**

February 18

Potchefstroom

South Africa A v Australians,
North West Cricket Stadium, Potchefstroom
Australians 8–351 (96 overs; RT Ponting 120, SR Waugh 91 not out)

I MUST ADMIT THAT BEFORE today's play began I felt a little bit nervous about my innings. I believed that how I went would have a major bearing on my tour from a personal point of view.

Yesterday was a solid start and my confidence had returned as quickly as it had been lost during moments of the recently completed Australian season. I also went out to bat remembering that during the past week my age has often been linked to a supposed loss of skills and know-how. What a load of crap — I am personally going to put this myth to bed. Concentration, as always, is going to be my key and I was determined to keep my approach as simple as possible. And by the end of the rain-interrupted day, where only 36 overs of play was possible, I felt rock solid, having reached 91 not out. As it turned out, the biggest danger today was posed not by any lack of form or focus but by the menacing thunderstorms and stunning bolts of lightning that lit up the skyline. It was good to be among the runs again, especially as I tend to gather momentum and keep it going once I get started.

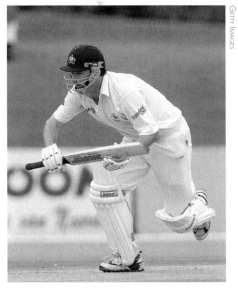

At the end of the day, the team's real-life soap drama turned another page with Warney and Binger having become embroiled in some kind of extortion case also involving the ACB. Shane gave the boys a run-down on the facts and what had happened, just to give us a 'heads up' before the press got to us, which was especially fortunate for me as I was just about to chat with them about today's play and

It would have been nice to reach a hundred before stumps, but given the ordinary weather getting to 91 and being unbeaten at stumps was an excellent way to start the tour.

any relevant issues. The pair are totally innocent. Warney must be sick of these distractions, and said as much when he commented on the ridiculous nature of the whole incident. Why, he asked, did it have to be him again?

Tonight was designated as a team night, with a BBQ and wine tasting the focus of our gathering. The team's resident wine expert, Stuart MacGill, initiated a question and answer contest involving all the boys. Each question had to be answered with a show of hands either placed on the head or attached to your backside. As the number of contestants decreased the questions became more difficult, until an eventual victor stood alone, which in this case was a surprised Mike Walsh, the team's cricket analyst and general workaholic. Lang took out round two and was rewarded with a bottle of the wine that he'd chosen earlier on. These nights are important for team unity, as they give each of us a genuine chance to get to know each other away from cricket.

February 19

Johannesburg

South Africa A v Australians,
North West Cricket Stadium, Potchefstroom
Australians 8–366 dec. (98.5 overs; SR Waugh 102 not out; AJ Hall 5–97) and 3–95 drew with South Africa A 190 (68 overs; AG Prince 92; GD McGrath 5–17)

AUSTRALIA WINNING TWO GOLD MEDALS at the Winter Olympics strongly suggests that anything is possible in life if you set your mind to it. Being away from home always makes you feel just that little bit more proud of anything Australian and the victories of Steven Bradbury and Alisa Camplin have become a real talking point among the boys.

Finally the rain clouds abated and today a full day's cricket was enjoyed by all. And what a great day it was for us. After posting my three figures to complete an innings that was for me a major plus — both mentally and from a technical point of view — we then bowled South Africa A out in 68 overs before finishing at 3 for 95 in our second dig. Our goals for the match had all been achieved, with plenty of good batting practice, the main bowlers all sending down about 15 overs each, and the boys running out the jet lag from the plane trip. Still, as hard as we played, the four reserves for the game — Watto, Magilla, Bic and Boof — probably worked the hardest during fitness tests conducted during the game by Jock Campbell. Jock is researching the effects of altitude on fatigue levels and used the boys as guinea pigs.

After a quick feed it was onto the bus, which for me wasn't a great option considering I have a facet joint problem in my lower back which was set off by a sudden movement when I cut a ball to reach my 100. Thankfully, the magic hands of Errol Alcott had already begun the rehabilitation process and the prognosis is looking positive.

Darren Lehmann, on the field as a substitute, congratulates Shane Warne, after the leg-spinner dismissed South Africa A's Andrew Hall.

The two-hour bus trip was made entertaining by the team's media manager Brian Murgatroyd, who read pages from *Full Time*, the autobiography of the former Irish soccer international Tony Cascarino. In this refreshingly honest book, Cascarino describes the little voice demons he had to fight during his career, a turmoil that plagues so many sportspeople and fills them with self-doubt.

February 20

Johannesburg

IT WAS TIME TO GET back on the physio's bench at 8.30am this morning, to establish whether or not I was going to need a facet block to negate

Directing traffic in Jo'burg, as we prepare for the first Test.

the pain I was experiencing, which appears to be caused by excess inflammation in my joints. Much to my relief the signs were encouraging and I had much more movement in all directions, even though it still felt as if I had been kicked by a mule with a bad temper. I'm hoping that by match morning — in two days' time — with the aid of the fast bowler's miracle red pills (Voltaren) I'll be close to 100 per cent fit.

A 10am team meeting was a real group effort. We split up into three groups, based on our batting order, to accumulate information on a variety of assigned subjects relating to our cricket and the upcoming Test, after which we regrouped to collate everything that we'd discussed and discovered.

This process provides us with an overall picture of how we want to play, what the conditions will be like and a brief résumé of the South Africans' danger players.

Our middle order group's message was blunt: let's embarrass them on their own turf. When I addressed the lads, my only words were to remind the team that we don't need an ICC trophy to tell us who the best team in the world is. We know we are the best, the South Africans know we are and that's all that counts. I want us to continue to be strong as a unit and to show the world how good we can be. And I ended by stressing the point that under relentless pressure South Africa will crack.

During our outdoor training session today, once again it was as if 'Ed TV' was the theme, as we had cameras intruding everywhere. Finally, they showed some respect and moved back to allow us an element of privacy.

Even with these distractions, the boys trained with an ever-increasing intensity and purpose as the session evolved. We all look ready to go.

Dinner tonight was at a Portuguese restaurant specialising in seafood, a somewhat ironic choice considering we are something like 2000 metres above sea level. But our memory of a previous visit is that it has on offer the best calamari in the world. The meal gave me another welcome opportunity to get to know Watto a little better, and as always Stuey MacGill was excellent company, with our conversation delving into a variety of topics. The passionate duo of Haydos and Lang rounded off the numbers and it must be said that a few bottles of local wine added to a very enjoyable evening.

February 21

Johannesburg

IT SEEMS AS IF EACH day brings a new scandal or headline associated with Australian cricket. From home comes the news that NSW batsman Graeme Rummans has tested positive to a masking agent which was found in urine samples that were taken routinely back in December. This was a major shock. Graeme is a good young bloke who has captained many under-age sides and has been earmarked for future honours.

After speaking with him and listening to his account of events, I'm sure he'll be given a sympathetic hearing. His mistake was to follow the advice of his local GP, who prescribed some medication to assist in the treatment of a boil on Graeme's shoulder, not realising that that medication contained a substance that is on the list of banned drugs. What needs to come out of this whole episode is a positive and that should be that every player's personal doctor needs to be in regular contact with the ACB and constantly updated about all banned or illegal substances so that they aren't ever administered.

It was optional training this morning and only a few players felt the need to hit the nets to finetune their games. This is indicative of the confidence in the camp and the relaxed mood that is permeating the squad. The scheduling of the official team photo shot ensured that we gathered together at the ground, enabling us to have a look at tomorrow's Test-match pitch. It looks a good one, with a fair covering of pale grass layered over a dryish looking base that is showing signs of cracking up. It looks a bat-first wicket to me.

As captain, today is press conference time, a regular pre-Test event that normally lasts about 15 to 20 minutes. This morning's affair wasn't all that confronting, but during it I was asked by a veteran ABC journalist if I was worried about losing my Test spot. I could only reply that last year I had averaged over 50 runs per innings in the calendar year and to me that wasn't too bad. Such questions make you wonder whether or not these guys actually do their homework. A more popular line of enquiry was how we all were mentally after the distractions of the past 10 or so days. The answer was easy: 'We are used to these distractions; in fact we wouldn't feel comfortable without them such is the spotlight we are always under. As professional cricketers, our job is to play the best we can and to meet our own high standards, because we want to remain the No. 1 Test side in the world.'

The 5.30pm match referee's meeting was its usual mundane self, even though the amiable Cammie Smith was running the show. The only surprise was that Mark Boucher and not Shaun Pollock was there as the South African captain. Pollock's side-strain hasn't healed satisfactorily, giving Boucher the ultimate honour in his 50th Test match. This must be a major disruption for the South Africans and I can already sense doubts creeping into their psyche. It's time to go for the jugular and give them a good hiding.

It was a movie night with room service for the cast of Lang, Haydos, Murgers and myself, as we settled in to watch the original *Rocky* — with Stallone at his best, delivering lines as only he can. Marto and Gilly popped their heads in to catch some gems from the 'Italian Stallion', before we all headed off to bed dreaming about our opponents and a potential knockout.

While I was stuck getting treatment on my back, most of the lads went to the Wanderers for a coaching clinic. Justin Langer, pictured here, was one of a number of guys who spoke of the promise and enthusiasm of the young cricketers from the Alexandria township that they met.

February 22

Johannesburg

South Africa v Australia, First Test,
New Wanderers Stadium, Johannesburg
Australia 5–331 (90 overs; JL Langer 28, ML Hayden 122, RT Ponting 39,
ME Waugh 53, SR Waugh 32, DR Martyn 21 not out, AC Gilchrist 25 not out)

THE BUS TRIP TO A Test-match venue on the first day is always a pensive one. Most players just stare out the window, not really taking in what's going on beyond the glass. We are preparing mentally for the battle ahead, just finetuning the mind and relaxing the body. Something I did notice was the variety of the animated gestures from the fans outside the ground, which strongly suggested that we were going to be in for a fair amount of verbal abuse and aggressive body language from the spectators over the next five days.

I know yesterday I'd come to the conclusion that it was a wicket on which I wanted us to bat first, but after I had another look at the deck this morning, I decided that in actual fact it wouldn't be too bad a toss to lose. The pitch still looked good to bat on, but it was also a fraction soft and contained some moisture. Stand-in captain Mark Boucher seemed especially keen to win the toss and after doing so quickly sent us in to bat. I felt that for South Africa this was a big gamble, given the state of their bowling attack — Allan Donald hasn't been at his best lately, Andre Nel is inexperienced and was bound to be nervous, Jacques Kallis has been lacking a yard of pace and their spinner, Nicky Boje, is a containing bowler rather than an attacking one. Makhaya Ntini looked to me to be their only in-form bowler and as such he carried an enormous burden. Bowling first, you must make early inroads or else you're in real trouble because you'll be batting last and probably chasing a big score to win.

This scenario was quite obvious to us, so we steeled ourselves for a big first-innings total. And, as it had been in the Tests in Australia, the top of the order was sensational, with Matthew Hayden scoring his fourth hundred in his last six Test innings (the other two were knocks of 3 not out and 21 not out). It was equal to any dig I've ever seen him play, primarily because the pitch played much harder than anyone expected. There was the springy bounce, plus enough sideways movement off the seam that it would have caused major problems under normal circumstances. However, the form of Haydos, Justin Langer, Ricky Ponting and Mark Waugh is unstoppable. Boundaries seemed to be coming every couple of balls, while the local boys were falling apart, with wayward bowling, dropped catches and poor field settings giving us the freedom to express ourselves.

I was welcomed at the crease by the now customary short ball, this one from Ntini. Expecting it to bounce a little more, I misjudged the elevation and copped it, at 145km/h, flush on the elbow. Initially, it didn't seem to hurt that much, but 10 seconds later I couldn't grip the bat and had sharp pains searing up and down my arm. When I risked a quick look, I saw a large lump growing by the second but I also knew instinctively that it wasn't broken, rather that I'd be wearing a severe bruise and probably had a lot of crushed nerves as well. After taking time to gather my composure, the next ball jagged back off the seam and crashed into my groin, bouncing off in the vicinity of the gully fielder.

This was a testing beginning, but at least I was awake to what was going on and the adrenalin was well and truly pumping.

Meanwhile, Haydos continued to slay them at the other end, crunching cover drives on the up — to the utter disbelief of Andre Nel, who had obviously never been treated with such contempt before. I can't imagine any batsman playing any better than Matthew is at the moment; he is simply awesome and will, in my mind, challenge Sachin Tendulkar for the mantle of the world's best batsman over the next couple of years.

Just when I was feeling settled in, I crashed a wide delivery from Kallis, only to find Herschelle Gibbs hovering in close at point to pull off a very good catch. Out for

Though only Matty Hayden went on to the big score, it was still a good day for all the batsmen in the Australian top seven. By stumps, Damien Martyn was 21 not out, having built a strong springboard for tomorrow.

32, a frustrating score as it means you did the hard work and were in a position to reap the rewards. My frustration was compounded when I was spat on by a South African supporter or a group of South African supporters on my way back to the dressing-rooms. The long walk back to the pavilion has a history of trouble, stemming from the fact that on each side you have rowdy spectators at close proximity and the trek is about 50 metres long. Merv Hughes tangled with a couple of loudmouths on our tour back in 1994, but the security lessons still haven't been learned.

Furious at copping a gob full of phlegm, I reported the incident to our manager, who promptly alerted the authorities, leading to the arrest of a man by the name of Elmo Stoop. Later on, Marto copped some full beers to the back of his head as he and Gilly came off at the end of an outstanding day for us. Scoring well over 300 in a day is no easy feat against any opposition; to do it on day one of a three-Test contest, and on such an awkward wicket, set an excellent tone for the remainder of this match and the rest of the series.

February 23

Johannesburg

South Africa v Australia, First Test,
New Wanderers Stadium, Johannesburg

Australia 9–652 dec. (146 overs; DR Martyn 133, AC Gilchrist 204 not out) v
South Africa 4–111 (32 overs: HH Gibbs 34, AG Prince 47 not out;
GD McGrath 2–27)

TODAY'S GAME PLAN REVOLVED AROUND scoring another 100 plus runs if possible. We believed that a total of around 450 would put real pressure on South Africa. What no one banked upon was the genius of Adam Gilchrist and the dependability of Damien Martyn. It was like watching four hours of non-stop highlights, as the boys massacred the best the South Africans could dish up.

Marto almost cantered to his hundred, barely taking a risk and doing it with ease. He really is in outstanding form, and totally in control of his

Adam Gilchrist in full flight – the best No. 7 batsman in world cricket today, maybe the best No. 7 there's ever been.

game and the methods he's employing. At the other end, Gilly was going so well and having so much fun that at one point he *nearly* took out the one-million-rand sign adjacent to the scoreboard. He slog-swept Boje so well that it missed the sign and sailed clean out of the ground. As strange as it may actually seem, before he played that shot we actually discussed what we would do if he hit the sign, such was our confidence in how sweetly he was hitting them. Our strategy was to throw it on either red or black at the Casino and then double it or lose it, which mightn't have pleased the guy doing the hard work — Gilly — but seemed pretty acceptable to we lads up in the stands.

When Marto was finally out for 133, after slicing a catch to third man, the pair had put on 317 for the sixth wicket, just 29 short of the world record set by Don Bradman and Jack Fingleton in the third Ashes Test of 1936–37. They'd batted for just 286 minutes, and faced 62.1 overs. Between lunch and tea Australia scored 190 runs, from 25.3 overs. Marto's second fifty took only 37 deliveries. Gilly slammed 98 runs in the middle session, having scored 76 between the start of play and lunch. It was unbelievable batting.

By tea time, Adam had reached 199 not out. Not wanting to be remembered for declaring on him, I elected to bat on to see him reach the quickest double hundred in Test history, which he achieved by hitting the first ball he faced when play resumed for four. He'd received just 212 balls, eight fewer than the previous record holder, Ian Botham, who'd seen 220 deliveries when he scored 208 against India at The Oval in 1982. We declared with Gilly 204 not out, from 213 deliveries, including 19 fours and eight towering sixes. He was only the fifth wicketkeeper to score a Test double century, and the first Australian keeper to achieve the feat.

Not only was Gilly's feat an extraordinary personal achievement, it lifted the mood of the squad to an even higher level, which wasn't a bad way to start our campaign with the ball. Everything went according to the script we had drawn up in our mind and put down on paper before the match. Most of the dismissals were as we had talked about, with the standout being Brett Lee's working over of Jacques Kallis during a memorable over. It was an awesome mix of short stuff perfectly zeroed in at the batsman's helmet combined with some searing yorkers. Kallis was in such a state that two balls before he was dismissed he let go a full-length ball that was missing the off stump by the width of a stump at the most. He was totally bamboozled and definitely expecting another short

For Shane Warne (ABOVE), working through a crowd at the airport at the start of a big tour is nothing new. But for a rookie such as Shane Watson (BELOW) this was just the start of a great new adventure.

ABOVE: **Stuey MacGill seems happily stunned at the potential of this budding leg-spinner.**
LEFT: **You might think this image is of me walking off after a batting failure. In fact, I've just made a hundred against South Africa A in Potchefstroom.**

Above: **The lads applaud as the runs continue to be piled on during the first Test in Jo'burg. This is widely regarded as being the most comfortable viewing area in world cricket.**
Below: **The three century-makers from our only innings of the first Test — Damien Martyn, Adam Gilchrist and Matthew Hayden — celebrate their achievement after our stunning victory.**

Both pics Steve Waugh

ABOVE: **These are the times you treasure. We're gathered together, arm in arm, ready to light up the tickets for the fourth and fifth days of the first Test.** LEFT: **And up they go! It looks like Watto's hair in the foreground, as he strains for a close-up look at the burning cardboard.**

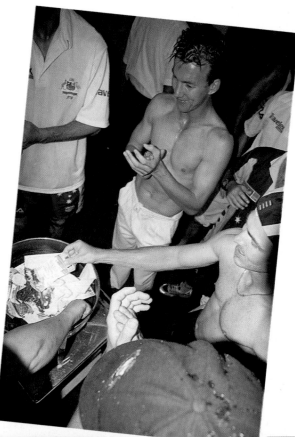

Two more angles of the incineration ceremony in the away dressing room at the Wanderers. Note the slightly damp baggy green in the foreground of the photograph at right.

ABOVE: **We're 1–0 up, but with plenty of work still to do.** BACK ROW, FROM LEFT: **Shane Watson, Ricky Ponting, Damien Martyn, Justin Langer, Steve Waugh, Glenn McGrath, Stuart MacGill.** MIDDLE: **Andy Bichel, Brett Lee, Jason Gillespie, Mark Waugh.** FRONT: **Darren Lehmann, Matthew Hayden, Adam Gilchrist.**
BELOW: **Right at this moment, immediately after the first Test, I was a very contented captain.**

ABOVE: **Being interviewed by police, after giving them my statement in order to begin criminal proceedings against a spectator who spat at me in Johannesburg. The main thing I was after was an apology, but I was also keen to send a message that this sort of behaviour by fans is not acceptable.** BELOW: **Celebration time for** (FROM LEFT) **Damien Martyn, Ricky Ponting and Shane Watson after our emphatic first Test win.**

ABOVE: **Captain and vice-captain savour the moment after the first Test in Jo'burg.**
BELOW: **Vice-captain and coach 'chew the fat' on the grass outside the change-rooms as the party inside continues.**

ball, and that's precisely what arrived at searing pace two balls later. All he could do was awkwardly fend it off to the safe hands of Shane Warne in the slip cordon.

This was more than just a key wicket, it sent out a message of intent to the rest of their side; that no one was safe and we were going after each and every batsman. By stumps we had them in real trouble, and we now genuinely believe that a victory might be possible by as early as tomorrow night.

Once again, the crowd was disappointing — both in its size and its behaviour. An especially crude banner aimed at Gilly caused some grief, requiring security to step in. At least we know what it feels like to be a Kiwi, after hearing all their endless sheep jokes and seeing ourselves being mimicked by some in the crowd doing unnatural acts to blow up sheep. The good news is that we reduced them to being very silent during the day, almost taking on the appearance of cardboard cutouts as they sat motionless for long periods at a time.

Brett Lee (arms raised) has just dismissed Jacques Kallis, as South Africa's reply to our massive first-innings total falters late on day two.

February 24

Johannesburg

**South Africa v Australia, First Test,
New Wanderers Stadium, Johannesburg**

Australia 9–652 dec. defeated South Africa 159 (48 overs: AG Prince 49;
GD McGrath 3–28, B Lee 3–40) and 133 (38.3 overs: HH Gibbs 47;
GD McGrath 5–21, SK Warne 4–44) by an innings and 360 runs

THIS MORNING WE KNEW THAT we could be facing a full day in the field —
if we could wrap up the South African tail quickly and send them in again
— so to conserve our energy we limited our warm-ups to a quick stretch,
catch and run around.

I couldn't help but have some memories of last year's Calcutta Test
against India, when we won a 274-run lead, sent them back in again and

Second-innings top-scorer Herschelle Gibbs is stumped by Adam Gilchrist off Shane Warne,
as South Africa crashes to its biggest ever defeat in Tests against Australia.

ended up losing the match. Here the conditions are much different and so is the strength of the batting line-up we are facing. The pitch here, with its bounce and movement, suits our quicks, whereas by day three the wicket in Calcutta resembled an airport runway. There also happens to be no Sachin Tendulkar or VVS Laxman capable of really damaging us, so I was inclined to enforce the follow-on again, so long as our bowlers hadn't bowled too many overs by the completion of the South Africans' first innings.

In fact, the locals meekly surrendered in 16 overs, so they were straight back in the firing line of a focused and hungry Aussie XI. Some 36 overs later, and No. 11 Allan Donald hobbled out with a runner (after damaging his hamstring in our first innings), only to be met by a barrage of short stuff. Not only was this the best way to get him out, it also indicated very decisively to our opponents that we weren't going to show any mercy by allowing even an incapacitated last man to get on the front foot. Shortly afterwards, he spooned a catch to gully and our huddle was joyous in its celebrations.

Judging by a gesture Donald made to the crowd, this will be his last Test, which brings to an end the magnificent career of a highly respected foe. We were also pleasantly surprised when we walked around the ground after the presentations to salute our supporters, because it was apparent that we actually have a significant following from many local fans. At times during the Test, when an element in the crowd were abusive and offensive, we hadn't realised that.

This was almost the perfect performance — exceptional batting, quality bowling and alert fielding. It was the second biggest winning margin by an innings in Test-match history, an achievement we all should be proud of. Needless to say, the party in the change-room was energetic, loud and sustained. But before I could switch to party mode I had to register a police report on the spitting incident from the other day, the culprit has been charged and if I want to proceed through the courts I had to make a statement. Marto followed suit, and then we settled in to savour our work over the past three days.

With the spectators now gone, Punter decided that our team song should be carried out in the caged walkway up from the field to the rooms. The rendition was rowdy and laced with emotion, and capped off by a celebratory 'retort' back at imaginary culprits. Further festivities continued in the dressing-rooms, with the burning of tickets for days four and five — pieces of cardboard that obviously aren't of much use any more. This may have been a touch arrogant, but at the time it seemed like

A Win for the Three Ps

This Australian team lives by the 'Three Ps' — partnerships, pressure and patience. And every one of those qualities was on show during our crushing win at the Wanderers.

When we batted, we put together partnerships, never falling into the trap of losing wickets in clusters the way we did in our two losses to India 12 months ago. Our ability to put together partnerships was a major factor during our Ashes triumph in England last year and it is always an indication that things are going well for us.

But more than batsmen just getting starts, you need them to go on and get three figures, and for the third time in four Tests three of our players made centuries. This allowed us to implement the second part of our plan — putting pressure on the opposition. The fact that we put so many runs on the board allowed us to set attacking fields; defending was not an issue. We could afford to have players in catching positions all the time and we could even experiment a little — like dispensing with fine leg and bringing him up to leg gully.

We also knew South Africa would feel the pressure as they were faced with a mammoth total in front of their fans. They had nothing to bat for except a draw and they needed to bat for an awfully long time just to do that.

That time we had led us to the third P in our plan — patience. With superb bowlers and plenty of time, we had to believe in our plans against each batsman, build the pressure, and wait for them to crack. That's exactly what happened — with devastating results.

A lot has been said about Adam Gilchrist's innings, and quite right too. It was a gem of a knock and one we'll never forget. When he is in that type of mood you realise you are watching a very special talent. But while celebrating Gilly's unique skills, we should never forget the contribution of Matthew Hayden on day one. He was again the man who laid the foundation for our victory, and he did so during what was actually an exceptionally difficult batting day. There was early moisture in the pitch, which led to plenty of sideways movement and also some really springy bounce, but Haydos was too good. When we batted first we needed players to stand up and be counted and that's exactly what Haydos — and the rest of the top seven — did admirably. Everyone went past 25 and occupied the crease.

This was a brilliant team effort. I'm sure at least part of it was a result of the relaxed attitude the players had during the build-up to the match. Our preparation may have been brief, with only one rain-affected lead-up match, but everything we did was focused, even down to the very short pre-Test team meeting.

We knew what we had to do and we went out and did it. No matter what individual records come our way, we are a team and the recognition of that fact was the basis for our great win here.

One of the keys to our great run in recent years has been the way we delight in each other's successes. Here the team mobs Glenn McGrath after one of his five second-innings wickets at the Wanderers.

a good idea, all in the name of fun. I hope all the boys realise just how special this result is and how good this side is, because I know that it hasn't always been this way and I also know that it definitely won't always be like this. I packed my gear a proud man, eagerly looking forward to squashing our arch enemy again in Cape Town.

February 25

Vanderbijlpark

HOW GOOD IS IT TO wake up on the morning of day four of a Test and be heading off not to the ground for warm ups but to a resort casino for a couple of days of rest and relaxation? I can tell you that if you've won the Test it is very good indeed. Before we could depart, I had to do a live cross to *A Current Affair* in Australia, who were able to confirm that our big win had been very well received at home. It's usually difficult to gauge the reaction of all Australians when you are touring and we never really know what the sentiments are until we start receiving media requests and are able to read newspaper articles that have been faxed to us. It's fantastic for the team to know how much support we have and it's something we really appreciate and value.

Emerald Safari Resort, situated at a place called Vanderbijlpark, about 90 minutes from Jo'burg, was the destination for the group of Justin Langer, Stuart MacGill, Brett Lee, Glenn McGrath, Shane Watson, Steve Waugh, John Buchanan, Errol Alcott, Lucy Frostick and Jock Campbell, while the others stayed in Jo'burg for a couple of days of golf on the local courses.

Our destination was reached by early morning, after a relaxed bus trip listening to the sounds of Moving Pictures, the Bee Gees and David Gray that filtered through the bus. It is unlikely Watto has heard of Moving Pictures, as he wasn't born while they enjoyed their big pub following in the early 1980s, but everyone knew the Bee Gees numbers. Lang tried to sell us on the smooth tones of David Gray, but his pitch was tempered a little when he mentioned to us that Gray 'wasn't bad for a Pom'.

After our journey, the day turned out to be a beauty, with a cruise down the Vaal River the highlight. We lazed on the top deck — throwing down the odd Red Bull and Vodka, and maybe a beer and Bacardi Breezer — oblivious to the fact we were turning crimson as the sun invaded our pale torsos and upper legs. After lunch it was time to partake in the water sports on offer, with McGrath taking up the challenge to stay atop of a floating rubber inflated object that was circular in shape and tied to a speedboat. Of course there was only one way this ride and every other subsequent journey was going to end — an unceremonious dumping at high speed. It didn't deter the boys, however, and culminated in Brett Lee being dragged through the backwash at serious speed before clipping a wave and being catapulted like a human cannonball into the air, soaring a good 10 metres before crashing and flipping over, much to the obvious delight of the boat operator. He explained, straight-faced, 'That's the best one I've seen for ages, look how far he went through the air!'

From here we then tried our hand at a couple of jet skis that nearly ended the tours of Binger and myself, after we almost collided at pace on

The crew at the Emerald Safari Resort, still on a high after the first Test. STANDING, FROM LEFT: **Lucy Frostick, Errol Alcott, Glenn McGrath, John Buchanan, Justin Langer.** CROUCHING: **Jock Campbell, Brett Lee, Steve Waugh and Shane Watson.**

our first lap of an imaginary racetrack. After surviving the water sports, our attention turned to a spot of fishing, with the allegedly huge local catfish our target. But not even the lure of a live frog on the end of our hooks could entice the '15kg plus' monsters to spring to life and we could only return to our lodges dreaming of what might have been.

Our dinner at the resort casino began nicely — thanks to a fine buffet meal featuring some gigantic T-bone steaks (which Pigeon for one didn't hold back on), washed down by a few more ales. This was followed by the consumption of a couple of 'shooters' each, to help Magilla celebrate his 31st birthday.

But then came a very unwelcome intrusion, with the news that a couple of guys with some paperwork from a South African drug-testing agency had tracked us down and wanted to straightaway do a test on Stuart MacGill and Shane Watson. Initially, we thought it was a hoax, and Buck and I went outside to check the legitimacy of their claims (after first up, I must confess, telling them via our security guy to get lost). A hoax it was not, but technically it was a bad joke for their forms said that they were required to perform the testing between February 27 and March 4. Today, of course, is February 25. The reason they were early, they explained, was that it was going to be difficult for them to get to us in Port Elizabeth over the next few days, so they thought they would suit themselves and bring the testing forward. That it messed up our night and no one could confirm whether or not it was actually all above board mattered little.

It was claimed they were acting on a directive from the Australian Sports Drug-testing Agency, but that didn't make sense because they had told us back in Australia before the tour began that they wouldn't be testing us while we were overseas.

Even after we made a number of phone calls, no one could say for certain what exactly was going on. I can't imagine the International Olympic Committee conducting testing in such an amateurish way, and I'm personally astounded by the whole episode. Thankfully, commonsense prevailed and the tests were delayed until the whole confusing mess could be sorted out.

Magilla's evening changed for the better on the blackjack table, where he had 10 rand on the long shot of being dealt three sevens in a row. It was high fives all round when they came up, a colossal winner that made it a night to remember even more than anyone could have imagined. Buck also tried his hand at blackjack, for the first time in his life, and was so bad he had the dealer laughing at his curious array of choices. Perhaps the play of the night came when Buck split his threes against the dealer's nine, a diabolical option.

Worse was to follow when another three appeared. He opted to continue the lunacy by splitting again, and as luck would have it was dealt yet another three — he had no option but to split again. He was now playing four hands against the dealer, and when he got a six to go with his last three it meant he could double up with one extra card, which of course he chose to do as we continued our hysterical laughter. The moment of truth arrived now ... with the dealer giving herself a six to go to 15 and give Buck the inside running on a miracle victory. However, lady luck had to run out and it did, ironically, when the dealer ended proceedings with a three.

Buck was left with just one winning hand, while the rest of us struggled to cope with our sore ribs.

February 26

Johannesburg

IT WAS OFF TO THE farm this morning to check out the lions, cheetahs and wild dogs to name but a few of the animals on show. This was followed by a 'game' drive, which was a little disappointing as we could only spot some deer and antelope. Afterwards, a BBQ by the campsite (featuring some more massive fillet steaks and snags, which seems to be the staple diet of all Africans) allowed us to keep our iron intake up.

Tonight's team meeting saw the boys in a jovial mood that was heightened by Buck's video of our trip, which he projected onto the meeting-room wall. One could say he didn't really capture the beauty, serenity and fun of the two days exactly as he would have liked, for the golf boys gave him an absolute hiding, confirming their belief that they made the right move in not coming along. It's fair to say that filming a tortoise for around 30 seconds isn't exactly riveting viewing, nor is the flight path of different species of birds in the aviary all that stimulating.

February 27

Port Elizabeth

AT 6.30AM IT WAS TIME to be up and among them, at a sportsmen's breakfast attended by around 800 people, with Shaun Pollock and me as the main attractions. All was going according to plan until I was about to make my way up onto the stage. At this point, however, the power source for the whole neighbourhood was shut down, leaving no electricity, no microphones, no lights and making it impossible for me to be seen or heard. With my bus to the airport due to leave in 30 minutes and the crowd getting increasingly agitated, desperate measures were called for. A loudhailer, it was decided, was the only option.

Answering questions in this way took me back to school days when we were being ordered into two straight lines by the teachers. Shaun and I both made the best of a difficult situation, which was further rescued by the microphones coming back on five minutes before the end. Despite all

Glenn McGrath and Mark Waugh arrive at our hotel in Port Elizabeth, to begin preparations for a game against a South Africa A side and then the second Test.

the difficulties, I must say that it was nice for a change to not be copping the tough and controversial questions. For now, they are all being directed my rival captain's way.

A gym and 'cardio' session was the extent of our training today, though a few of us did go down to the ground for a quick net session. The upcoming match against another South Africa A combination should provide the four guys who missed the first Test an opportunity to display their skills and for each of them to keep pushing for a Test berth of his own. It will be especially exciting to watch Shane Watson make his international debut.

February 28

Port Elizabeth

AFTER OUR SHORT BREAK, IT was good to get back into the serious business of a full-scale net session. The effort and intensity of everyone was encouraging, as we look ahead to our upcoming matches. What we must not do now is read too much of the press and start believing the series is a foregone conclusion, because top-level sport can bite you real quick if you ever become complacent and lazy.

There are certainly times, when you're away from home, when you miss out on important moments in your family's life. Speaking to Lynette this morning she informed me that our baby Lillian has rolled over for the first time. This made me feel instantly homesick, because she had been threatening to do it for a while now and I had hoped to be there when it happened. But life goes on; as a professional sportsman I have to accept that sacrifices must be made to achieve the results everyone in the squad wants.

A walk along the beach directly in front of our hotel helped clear the head and relax the mind and body. Hearing the sound of crashing waves and children laughing is a combination that reminds me of summer in Australia and with the fresh sea breeze it provided a cocktail of tranquility that was a welcome diversion from the pressure of the tour.

A team dinner at the Casino was sumptuous, and the right price, too, but most of us paid for it many times over at the gambling tables later on.

March 1

Port Elizabeth

South Africa A v Australians, St George's Park, Port Elizabeth
South Africa A 7–288 (88 overs: DJ Cullinan 86, HM Amla 81) v Australians

I WAS PLEASED TO HEAR this morning that there had been some good news for Graeme Rummans, who received a one-month ban and a fine in relation to his positive drug test. Following a hearing that apparently went for close to eight hours, a specialist panel found that Graeme had breached his responsibilities under the terms of the ACB's Anti-Doping Policy, but it was also established that he had not gained or sought to gain an unfair advantage over other players in taking the substance. Consequently, sympathy was shown, for which I am thankful, especially so because I told Brett Lee that if Graeme got the maximum two-year ban I was going to shave my head in protest. This would have been embarrassing, for I'm sure the kids wouldn't have recognised me and the dents on top of my skull would not have been too aesthetically pleasing for anyone.

Winning the toss today provided me with a bit of a dilemma, because the correct decision would have been to bat on a dead-looking pitch. Instead, I chose to field first, for two reasons — I wanted us to stay in a winning mode and to do this we must take 20 wickets, so why not start straight away, and I also wanted to give Andy Bichel, Stuart MacGill and Shane Watson a good workout at the bowling crease as it may be their only game on tour and thus represented an important opportunity for them.

At tea time, things weren't looking too rosy for us, but to the team's credit we hung in there and by close had probably won the day with South Africa A finishing at 7–288, made on not only a favourable pitch but with a lightning fast outfield offering the batsmen further assistance.

The most significant innings of the day came from Daryll Cullinan, whose effort will I'm sure be enough to see him earn a Test recall. He played very well, as we know he can, but as soon as we get him in a Test match scenario he'll immediately have some self-doubts, especially when facing Warney. These doubts will, I believe, override his natural abilities and drag him down. Only time will tell, and the great thing about every sport is that anything is possible, as long as you truly believe you can do it.

Watto's debut was very encouraging. As I watched him bowl from my fielding position in the covers I was struck by how much he reminded me of the former Bankstown, NSW and Australian paceman Len Pascoe in his action. He is strong, enthusiastic and very competitive — all traits that will stand him in good stead.

This match is very important for the side, because we must sustain the momentum created by our great win in the first Test. You can't let this sort of impetus slip, as it may not come back. The four reserves for this match — Warney, Haydos, Marto and Pigeon — all took turns at the 12th-man duties, and also fitted in a gym session with Jock to help prepare themselves for the Cape Town Test. The fitness levels have been an important ingredient in our success and Jock, the 'boy from Mt Druitt', relishes his work, though lately I've been wondering whether he's been training extra hard to punish himself for the awful 'Midnight Express' haircut he actually paid for during the tour's early days.

March 2

Port Elizabeth

South Africa A v Australians, St George's Park, Port Elizabeth
South Africa A 301 (92.3 overs: B Lee 4–37) v Australians 5–452
(97 overs: JL Langer 161, DS Lehmann 60, RT Ponting 40, ME Waugh 110,
SR Watson 20 not out, AC Gilchrist 38 not out)

THE PERFECT ENDING CAME ABOUT this morning with three quick wickets to wrap up the South Africa A innings. It was now our turn to settle in and hopefully make a big score on a flat pitch with a quick outfield and some small boundaries. Our plan was to bat well and only once, then get the opposition back in and win in three days to give us a day off. This is a four-day game instead of the usual (for a tour game) three, which to me is

Darren Lehmann on his way to 60 on day two of our game against South Africa A in Port Elizabeth.

plenty long enough. Somehow, this one slipped through the pre-itinerary draft without being spotted.

Thanks to a well-crafted century from Justin Langer and a fine exhibition of strokeplay from Mark Waugh that saw him reach three figures too, we literally smashed their Test hopefuls all over the park. The only exception to this was a young quick named Dewald Pretorius, who impressed with his pace and bounce. What an inspiration he will be to many kids of the future, as he grew up an orphan but overcome this tough start to now excel in his chosen field.

After waiting round for the better part of the day with the pads on, I finally got my chance with about 10 overs remaining in the day and the second new ball shining in the quicks' hands. Before I had scored, Lang was out for 161, which meant that the 'Ken doll' (Shane Watson — Bing thought this would be a good nickname for his young buddy) took strike at the other end. He was obviously quite nervous, but the gods smiled upon him when he edged his very first ball but was given not out, much to the bowling team's disgust and our relief. However, 'justice' was just around the corner for them, because I was given out next over, caught behind, when I believe I missed the ball. It has been said that cricket is a great leveller, but I can't subscribe to that theory at the moment.

Not having done any exercise today, after play I made the 40-minute walk home from the ground, and was accompanied by Lang, Gilly, Jock, Lucy and Hooter. It was a nice way to alleviate the stress and give the body some kind of work.

Taking me back to my youth tonight was a game of Monopoly, played between Murgers (a connoisseur of the game), Magilla (a ruthless accumulator of assets), Dizzy (the Ebenezer Scrooge of play money) and Boof (the cagey, observant one) in the team room. This war of attrition was fierce, while the tactical acumen of the quartet was tested, but in the end it was the hard-headed, cold-blooded greed and manipulative qualities of Magilla that shone through and saw him crush his foes with clinical efficiency. There was no room for the faint-hearted, as the pre-game favourite — who had honed his lifelong skills in Cardiff before becoming the ACB Media Manager — found out in no uncertain terms. Murgers attributed his early departure to the fact that the streets were South African and not from England, but we all knew he had simply acquired the wrong assets and played his hand poorly. The poor fellow was a shattered man as he packed away his now useless pieces and hauled himself back to his room to have a look at himself in front of the mirror.

March 3

Shamwari Game Reserve

South Africa A v Australians, St George's Park, Port Elizabeth

South Africa A 301 and 232 (60.3 overs: JM Kemp 56, GH Bodi 45;
SCG MacGill 4–114, AJ Bichel 3–41) lost to Australians 9–574 dec. (116.2 overs:
SR Watson 100 not out, AC Gilchrist 56) by an innings and 41 runs

WATTO CAME OUT BLAZING, AS did Gilly, in line with my instructions to try to score a quick 150 and then send them back in. As is often the case, even the best-laid plans can come unstuck, because while our target was achieved in tremendous time, the debutant was nearing a hundred, which would represent a notable achievement and provide a lift for the whole squad. So our declaration was delayed to allow the young Tasmanian to reach his century with a six, which made it even more memorable. Watto appears to

Not too many cricketers have scored 100 in their debut tour game for Australia. Fewer still have done so off just 97 balls, as Shane Watson did here.

ABOVE: **It's early morning and the lads are on a game drive through the Shamwari Game Reserve, in search of a giraffe or two.**

BELOW: **Lang takes the role of barman on a cruise up the Vaal River, near Vanderbijlpark. In the background are Jock and Lucy, enjoying themselves away from the grind of touring life.**

ABOVE: **The lads take the chance to relax while sunning themselves as we cruise up the impressive Vaal River.**
LEFT: **Buck, great big kid that he is, takes to the water.**

BELOW: **Lang and Watto test out the jet skis, while in the foreground a frog hangs from a fishing line, waiting for another attempt to land an elusive catfish.**

Fishing — with absolutely no joy —
for giant catfish on the Vaal River.
Perhaps our various techniques
needed revising?

There's nothing quite like the wild animals of Africa.

One of my favourite animals is the languid, graceful and occasionally well-disguised giraffe.

ABOVE: **In a few moments we will be beginning our firefighting careers, as a back-burning operation goes wrong on a neighbouring property to Bayethe Lodge, near Port Elizabeth.**
BELOW: **Lang gets stuck in with a high-tech piece of firefighting equipment — a cut-down bush.**

Our expedition to Robben Island was a tour highlight. At right, Justin Langer checks out the cell that once held Nelson Mandela, while below our tour guide — who was once a prisoner here — gives us a fantastic insight into what existence was about 'on the inside'. It was called, in his words, the 'University of Life'.

ABOVE: **Arriving at Robben Island. Luckily, we were in the right queue.**
BELOW: **The limestone mines at Robben Island, which came back to haunt the inmates who worked in them. Chiselling into the deposits brought each and every prisoner eye problems that afflicted them later in life.**

Adam Gilchrist, Justin Langer (holding helmet), Ricky Ponting and Andy Bichel (in white hat) move in to congratulate Stuart MacGill on bowling Martin van Jaarsveld during South Africa A's second innings.

have the power of a Simon O'Donnell and it looks to me as if Australian cricket may just have found the genuine all rounder it has been searching for. It's terrific to see a young talent performing in this way, and the future of Australian cricket is looking good if this is the sort of talent that is around.

Now for the hard work — bowling out the opposition on a flat wicket. Again, our professionalism shone through. Often these tour games can become lifeless affairs, especially if the team becomes negative or loses its focus. In my view, this is where mental toughness is attained. If you can discipline yourself when nothing much in the way of rewards is at stake, then you won't have any trouble reproducing when you are alert, excited and energised by a challenge.

Brett Lee was very powerful in his action and impressed with the pace he generated. He looks set for a strong tour, as he gets back to his best after the serious elbow injury he suffered 12 months ago. After getting through some tough periods in the day we ended up achieving our target for the match, much to everyone's joy, especially so as Haydos had

Australian teams always enjoy snaring the wicket of Daryll Cullinan. This time, Andy Bichel did the damage, trapping Cullinan lbw.

organised a trip for the lads to the Shamwari Game Reserve. The first choice of Sun City was totally booked out, which was a real downer because each of the last two tours we've had to South Africa have provided us with memorable bus trips to this exotic location.

Half a dozen of us ended up making the drive to Bayethe Lodge located in the Reserve, to have drinks around the campfire and dinner under the stars. A couple of interesting choices were on offer for dinner — slices of springbok, à la sushi style, and grilled ostrich — which tempted both Pigeon and Magilla, but not the rest of the lads, who preferred chicken spring rolls and grilled fish. Then we embarked on a night game drive that unfortunately revealed little of the animals we hoped to see.

Still, there's something about unpolluted air, especially in Africa, that makes you feel alive and invigorated. Nature is wonderful and should never be taken for granted.

March 4

Port Elizabeth

FINISHING OUR NIGHT DRIVE AT 1am suddenly seemed like a poor tactical move when we were up and at 'em at 5.45am for a morning game drive. However, lady luck was on our side this time with a pair of white rhinos, an assortment of antelope and half a dozen giraffe coming close to our open-topped vehicle. For Buck, an aspiring Cecil B de Mille, it was a disaster, with his trusted video recorder going haywire just when he spotted his favourite animal (and also the closest looking animal relative to himself), the giraffe. No matter how many buttons he pressed and willed to work, it wouldn't come to life and it's as close as I've seen a grown man cry without actually shedding tears.

All good things must come to an end, but before we had to head back for training there was a window of opportunity to either catch up on sleep — as Watto, Bing and Haydos opted for — or laze around and have a chat, which Lang, Pigeon and myself did. Talk about the wrong option. Suddenly, we became aware of the unwanted sight of hazy smoke billowing up from the horizon. The smoke meant fire, and with a reserve full of expensive wildlife, thatched cottages, and dry bush and vegetation, the smoke meant immediate danger. Wanting to be of assistance, we volunteered to roll up the sleeves and do our bit, but as we got closer to the outbreak this looked to be a bad move.

Upon arrival at the fire, we quickly realised that there weren't any of the items usually associated with fighting fires — things such as such as water trucks, hoses or firemen. Instead, our only tools were machetes, to be used to cut branches which would be used to put out the fire. Belting flames out with these branches, and also sandals, shorts and nylon tops, didn't offer us any great protection from the sweltering heat, but McGrath was right in his element, almost as if he was back at 'Woncobra', his property in outback New South Wales. Lang was, as always, enthusiastic and right among the action, while I did my best to be useful and not catch on fire. Eventually, thanks to a drop in the breeze and some help from a nearby lodge — which had a ute with makeshift firefighting equipment on the back of it — the situation was brought under control. This was a unique warm-up before our team training session.

The highlight of our training session was the presence of Gareth, a 10-year-old boy who has brightened our time up here in Port Elizabeth during the past four or five days. Gareth suffers from dwarfism, but has an attitude and love of life that are infectious and inspirational. To see him play touch footy was to recognise that he doesn't have a disability but rather a gift. Watching him score the winning try was a wonderful way to end the fun of training before heading off for a 45-minute fielding workout.

Mark Waugh meets the press after learning he'll be joining me on the sidelines for the one-day internationals that follow this Test tour.

March 5

Cape Town

MAKING USE OF THE BEACHFRONT was a fair way to start the day. Gilly, Marto, Jock and I spent an hour or so walking, running and swimming on a near-deserted beach before we joined the boys for breakfast. I thought I went OK, but as Jock often says to me, 'Your grandmother works out better than that.'

Confusion surrounded our arrival in Cape Town due to the fact that the South Africans had booted us out of the Cullinan Hotel, because they didn't want us in the same pub as themselves. What a load of 'bollocks' and an obvious play to unsettle us before the Test. In Australia, we regularly stay in the same hotel as our opponents and no one seems to care. Our new address had rooms of very minimal size, which normally wouldn't present any problem, but as most of the wives and girlfriends arrive in town tonight it is disappointing that this has occurred.

Tonight's vineyard excursion was very enjoyable and rather unique — besides a three-course meal that saw us swap seats after each course, and a tour of the winery accompanied by a wine-testing session, we had a major treat. A photo session with a cheetah restrained only by what looked like a dog leash was a big adrenalin rush. To be able to pat a fully-grown animal like this gives you a greater appreciation of its strength and beauty and gets the heart rate up a fair percentage.

March 6

Cape Town

THE BIG NEWS TODAY HAS been the withdrawal from the South African team of Daryll Cullinan. Citing differences of opinion with the South African Cricket Board over contractual issues, he decided to pull out, and received universal condemnation from his countrymen. Surely his

Every net session was a chance to reaffirm that while the runs weren't coming in big numbers out in the middle, I actually was hitting the ball pretty well.

situation could have been sorted out before it reached this stage? I find it amazing that someone who has been out of the side for an extended period, who was desperate to get back in finally cracks it for a comeback but then walks away over money. Surely he has a reason to do this and hopefully in time the reason for his decision will be made clearer and then the decision will be accepted a lot better. Perhaps he is leading a battle on behalf of others, but the overwhelming sentiment at the moment is that he's selfish and worried only about himself. Whatever the rights and wrongs, it's a real shame for everyone, especially Warney, who fancied taking Cullinan's scalp again to help celebrate his 100th Test.

With Shaun Pollock continuing to be unavailable due to injury, the locals do not hold out much hope for their team. Everyone thinks it'll be a walk in the park for us.

Our team meeting was again short and simple. When things are going well there is no need to overanalyse or talk in circles. The key messages for this Test are again to show respect for the opposition, follow the 3 Ps — patience, pressure, partnerships — keep our standards high and focus on the cricket by blocking out any distractions.

We enjoyed a helicopter ride around the cape, which was quite awesome as the doors of the Army helicopter stayed open, leaving us to gaze out at the majestic scenery with only a seat belt for protection. Stuey MacGill, being very uncomfortable with heights, took on his fear and prevailed … but only just. It was a memorable trip and we were all grateful to the locals who looked after us.

Following a pre-match routine that has worked for me in the past, I had a massage/physio session and a good feed to get me in the mood for — hopefully — another big Test. Capping off an excellent day was the sight of a photo album of the kids that brother Mark's partner Sue brought me over. Seeing these photos — and the way the children literally grow up before my eyes — is both exciting and depressing. My kids bring so much joy and love into my life, and I can often feel somewhat cheated that I'm not there for everything. But then reality kicks in — I know that life goes on and that there's a job to do here right now.

Adam Gilchrist goes back to his days as a New South Welshman, as he cuts between Jock Campbell and Justin Langer, with Shane Watson in the background.

March 7

Cape Town

IN THE AUSTRALIAN SET-UP, THE day before a Test now features a non-compulsory net session. Usually, it is attended by most of the batsmen, who benefit from an extra hit courtesy of net bowlers, and today the guys who sent down the deliveries provided an excellent workout.

On a personal note, I feel a big score is imminent as I'm striking the ball well and can sense a significant innings is brewing. The bowlers, with the exception of Shane Watson, went through a gym session followed by a massage to finish off their preparations for a Test everyone expects us to win and win comfortably. Of course, it's not quite so easy. I'm sure the three new caps in the Proteas side will inject plenty of enthusiasm into their line-up and present us with that 'unknown' factor that we must never underestimate.

As captain, the day before a Test can be busy when it comes to media obligations. Today I did a radio interview back to Australia, a five-minute interview for the host TV broadcaster and a press conference for both the South African and Australian media contingents.

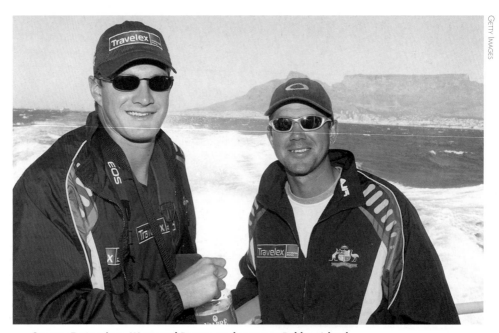

Our two Tasmanians, Watto and Punter, on the way to Robben Island.

Warney, 100 not out!

I remember saying to myself, 'Who's this guy and where has he come from?' During an Australia B tour of Zimbabwe just over a decade ago, I first laid my eyes upon a man I instantly saw as a genius with the ball.

You could actually hear the ball buzzing its way through the air once it left the young man's Havana cigar-like fingers, such were the energy and revolutions he put on the ball. His delivery was angry, ferocious and aggressive, purely mesmerising in its beauty and execution. In short, he had just about the perfect leg-spinning action and a once-in-a-lifetime skill, combined with an inbuilt know-how and instinct for a duel. He seemed almost like a genetically created machine capable of inflicting anarchy on its opponents.

In his first 99 Test matches, Shane Warne has fulfilled that exceptional promise to be named as one of *Wisden's* five best cricketers of the 20th century, as well as making Australia's Team of the Century.

It hasn't, however, been all fairy floss and show bags along the way. Being such a high-profile figure who is both marketable and magnetic, Shane has found himself embroiled in a number of controversies that have ensured that he has kept plenty of fish and chips warm over the years.

One of Shane's traits that is often overlooked, yet I believe has been the key to his longevity and prosperity in the game, is his resilience to all the obstacles which have presented themselves. He has overcome career-threatening injuries, loss of form, controversy and competition to come out the other side stronger, and more determined and focused on what he wants to achieve.

He has always wanted to be the best and is forever on the lookout for ways to stay one step ahead. Warney can often be seen working on a new ball which might only be slightly different, but it will be unique and perfectly executed when it is revealed to the world.

As a bowler he is candidly plotting, scheming and analysing his opponent to try to establish a chink in his armour. His body language is often very dominant, establishing a pecking order in the middle that sees a batsman very low down in the food chain.

Food, it must be said, is not one of Warney's great strengths, but toasted cheese sandwiches, spaghetti bolognese and pizza may well be his secret vitamin source. It could be that it is the rest of us who are the ones whose thinking on nutrition is wrong. This said, fitness is an area Shane has recently targeted, and the results have been very noticeable. For Australia's sake, this is an excellent sign for the future.

All great players love a challenge and are stimulated by the need to always improve. Shane is no exception to this rule, especially when it comes to his batting. He has really knuckled down this Australian season, as evidenced by his dramatic 99 in the Test against New Zealand in Perth. To his credit, he has disciplined himself in the art of concentration, which in the past he has lacked. This is understandable when you consider the colossal amount of bowling he does and the application that is associated with getting that process right every ball. In the past, batting has been his outlet and freedom, but he has decided that runs on the board are what counts, and his improvement has been a terrific example to those around him.

Shane brings up his century of Tests in the second Test that begins tomorrow, a great achievement, and I feel privileged to have been a part of most of his ton. Knowing Warney and his gift for producing on the big stage, I feel something special is in store for Cape Town.

CRICKETERS WHO HAVE PLAYED 80 TESTS AND TAKEN 100 TEST WICKETS
As at March 6, 2002

Name	Mat	Runs	Ave	Wkts	Ave	Ct
CA Walsh (WI)	132	936	7.54	519	24.44	29
Kapil Dev (Ind)	131	5248	31.05	434	29.64	64
Wasim Akram (Pak)	104	2898	22.64	414	23.62	44
IT Botham (Eng)	102	5200	33.54	383	28.40	120
SK Warne (Aus)	**99**	**1974**	**16.04**	**436**	**26.52**	**80**
CEL Ambrose (WI)	98	1439	12.40	405	20.99	18
GS Sobers (WI)	93	8032	57.78	235	34.03	109
CL Hooper (WI)	92	5020	35.10	103	50.13	106
RGD Willis (Eng)	90	840	11.50	325	25.20	39
Imran Khan (Pak)	88	3807	37.69	362	22.81	28
RJ Hadlee (NZ)	86	3124	27.16	431	22.30	39
DL Underwood (Eng)	86	937	11.56	297	25.83	44
GD McGrath (Aus)	82	405	6.63	385	21.67	24

It was our good fortune after training to visit, via ferry, Robben Island — the isolated landmass that housed many political prisoners of the apartheid era, including Nelson Mandela. My admiration for this great man grows each and every day I learn more about him. To be locked up for 27 years and then to have your freedom returned to you — and to not hold any grudges or resentment — is quite amazing. To take a positive stance and to see the bigger picture indeed takes an extraordinary amount of vision and courage.

Our guided tour was highlighted by an informative talk from a young man who had spent five years of his life incarcerated on the island. His behind-the-scenes account of daily existence and what living on this island involved were inspirational. What struck me most was the attitude of the prisoners, how they wanted to better themselves by learning and sharing information — which was abundant given that so many of the people locked up on the island were highly-qualified professionals from various walks of life.

Stuart MacGill again came through in the eating department, finally securing a restaurant at his 10th attempt. Cape Town at the moment is fully booked out, with the Test cricket, Super 12 rugby and the Cape Argus (cycle tour) attracting thousands of visitors to this beautiful city.

With Glenn McGrath and a tour guide inside what used to be Nelson Mandela's cell at the stark, dreadful yet fascinating Robben Island.

March 8

Cape Town

South Africa v Australia, Second Test, Newlands, Cape Town

South Africa 239 (80 overs: AJ Hall 70; GD McGrath 3–42, JN Gillespie 3–52) v Australia 0–46 (8 overs: JL Langer 28 not out, ML Hayden 17 not out)

IT WAS AN AIR OF quiet confidence and optimism that filled the bus on our 15-minute trip to the ground for the start of today's second Test. At the ground, I made one last pitch inspection which confirmed a thought that had been in my head since the first time I set eyes on the Test wicket — that this would be a toss that I wouldn't mind losing. And lose it I did.

I always call heads, a strategy that has been kind to me during my career as a Test-match captain. This was quite obviously a bat-first wicket, but despite this — after the double failure in Johannesburg — I was also keen to bowl first and put their batsmen under pressure. Cricket is such a mental game that sometimes it doesn't even matter what the conditions are, it's more about the two teams' states of mind.

Our catching today was phenomenal. Two highlights were Gilly's diving one-handers to either side of the wicket, which demonstrated how his keeping skills continue to be underrated. Or maybe they're simply overshadowed by his exceptional batting. In all, nine catches were held in the slip cordon, which stayed in place throughout the innings and gave the batsmen no respite or relief; they knew that any slight mistake would be pounced upon. Of course, for me to set these highly attacking fields we need highly disciplined and highly skilful bowlers who are capable of executing impeccable line and length.

Late in the day, the batting of Langer and Hayden was again outstanding, with 46 coming from eight overs to send out a clear message that we want to continue the momentum and incessant pressure our cricket is placing on our opponents. New boy Dewald Pretorius went for 33 off three overs and must be wondering what this Test-match cricket is all about. It was no coincidence that he went for 11 per over, as Lang had targeted him. This was bold, courageous batting and another example of this man's development as a batsman of the highest class.

Shane Warne, latest graduate to the '100 Test' club, talks to another member in Cape Town.

A trip to Newlands rugby stadium rounded off the day. It is an awesome stadium, where we were part of a highly motivated and parochial crowd who saw the local Stormers home to an easy win against a Hurricanes side that included the intimidating presence of Jonah Lomu.

March 9

Cape Town

South Africa v Australia, Second Test, Newlands, Cape Town

South Africa 239 and 0–7 (five overs) v Australia 382 (80.5 overs: JL Langer 37, ML Hayden 63, RT Ponting 47, AC Gilchrist 138 not out, SK Warne 63; M Ntini 4–93, PR Adams 4–102)

IT REALLY IS A PLEASURE to play at Newlands, with the majestic Table Top Mountain dominating the surrounding landscape and giving the venue an air of immortality. What an appropriate venue for another day of Test cricket dominated by the freakish skills and sense of occasion that only Adam Gilchrist seems able to provide. Watching on from the sidelines, I've reached the stage that I can almost pick up his mood and where the next ball is going to be dispatched. He is a perfect example of dominating body language when he's in form, something the opposition senses and fears. For clean hitting, only a couple of batsmen of recent times spring to mind — and both Sir Vivian Richards and Ian Botham are legends of the game, a path our custodian is bound to follow.

For me, today turned out to be another examination of my resolve to hang in there and turn things around, after I succumbed to the competitiveness and craziness of Paul Adams. After a solid lead-up of net sessions and throw downs, I was determined in my mind to be as positive as possible and to back myself no matter the situation. In the quest to get my score moving I fell to a cardinal sin for any batsman — I worried more about the outcome than the process, which equates to failure.

Trying to get to 20 quickly sounded like a good plan, but in targeting this I forgot to have a good look at the conditions of the pitch, how it was bouncing, what pace it was and what variations the bowler was capable of. I was keen to force Adams down the ground

Makhaya Ntini, who in the absence of the injured Allan Donald and Shaun Pollock became the leader of the South African pace attack.

The Tiger Woods of Cricket

Rarely, if ever, has a cricketer had such a profound effect on the outcome of matches, particularly at the start of his career, as has Adam Gilchrist. Gilly has been part of 24 winning Test matches out of 30, was the quickest wicketkeeper to 100 dismissals in Test history, and has scored six of the greatest centuries that have ever been made.

Surely it is time for him to retire, for this can't possibly continue. Or can it? Under normal circumstances this would be a fair assumption, but Gilly is not your average international player. In fact, he may end up one of the all-time great players. The only thing capable of stopping him in his tracks at the moment is a chunk of kryptonite, such is his momentum and confidence.

It is difficult to bracket him alongside any other player I have seen, but Viv Richards would be the closest to him for the freedom and expression of skills and the pure essence of what batting is all about. To Gilly (as it was for Sir Viv), each ball is seen as an opportunity to score a boundary, rather than a chance to be dismissed. And Gilly plays the same way no matter the circumstances of the match situation, conditions or opposition.

He has a grip that is probably a little unconventional, in that he holds the bat higher up the handle than most — which gives him a fuller, longer swing like a John Daly or Tiger Woods in golf. He also has an impeccable eye and a natural gift for timing. Very often, the opposition fieldsmen are caught out by the speed at which the ball is coming at them. This deception is caused by a combination of strong forearms and wrists, which send the ball on its way at often lightning speed.

Obviously, to play this way takes a lot of skill and self-belief, qualities one needs to succeed at the top level.

Adam has already shown he possesses mental toughness by stepping into Ian Healy's shoes, which many would have baulked at.

While Gilly is a freak of a talent, his great strength to me is his sense of team and the compassion he shows to others.

Adam Gilchrist goes over the top during what became the fastest double century ever scored in Test cricket.

ABOVE: **Always a treasured moment — that first hundred for Australia. This one of Shane Watson's against a South Africa A side in Port Elizabeth was all the more memorable because it came on his debut and came in a real hurry, too. Behind Watto, Brett Lee can't hide his joy that one of the new brigade has come good.**

BELOW: **Lang is in charge of the music after we wrapped up the series in magnificent fashion in Cape Town. Below him, Bic and Punter talk through the fairytale ending to a memorable Test match.**

A tale of two centuries.
RIGHT: **Ricky Ponting smiles**
for my camera after his
superb match-winning
century at Newlands.
BELOW: **Adam Gilchrist has**
just scored the fastest
double century in Test
history, but after the
declaration, he has to
quickly change from batting
to keeping pads. Still, you
can't keep the satisfied grin
from Gilly's face, a fact that
will be just as clear in
Buck's home video as it is in
this photograph.

Two photographs of the visitors' dressing-room at the Wanderers. In the shot BELOW, it's time to celebrate after our near-perfect performance in the first Test. Haydos (LEFT) ices up those knees, while Dizzy (with ice behind the left ankle) and Pigeon enjoy a cold one, and Gilly's man-of-the-match trophy (in the foreground) 'listens in'.

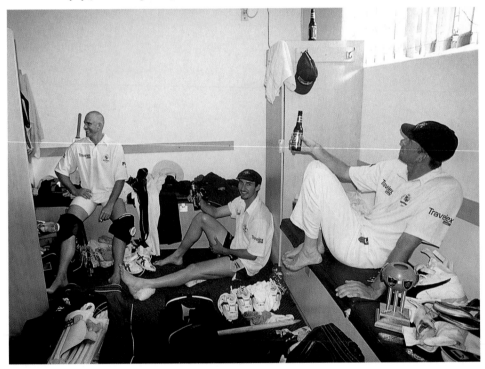

ABOVE: **Justin Langer talks about one of his favourite people, Nelson Mandela, on the island where the great man was incarcerated for 27 years before his release in 1990.**
BELOW: **Six graduates of the Australian Cricket Academy pay tribute to long-time head of the Academy Rod Marsh after it was announced that the former Test wicketkeeper would be leaving the Academy in Adelaide to take up a similar coaching job in England.**

ABOVE: **Thanks to the generosity of the locals, we had the use of two choppers for an afternoon's sightseeing over Cape Town.**
LEFT: **The smiles undoubtedly hide the true feelings of Darren Lehmann** (RIGHT) **and Stuart MacGill** (CENTRE), **especially the latter, who has a fear of heights. Errol Alcott is to Magilla's right.**
BELOW: **Rounding the tip of Cape Town offers a majestic sight.**

ABOVE: **An aerial shot of the Newlands rugby stadium in Cape Town, with the cricket ground in the background.**
RIGHT: **A few of the lads (Gilly, Buck, Lang, Haydos and me) are introduced to a baby kudu at Bayethe Lodge, near Port Elizabeth.**

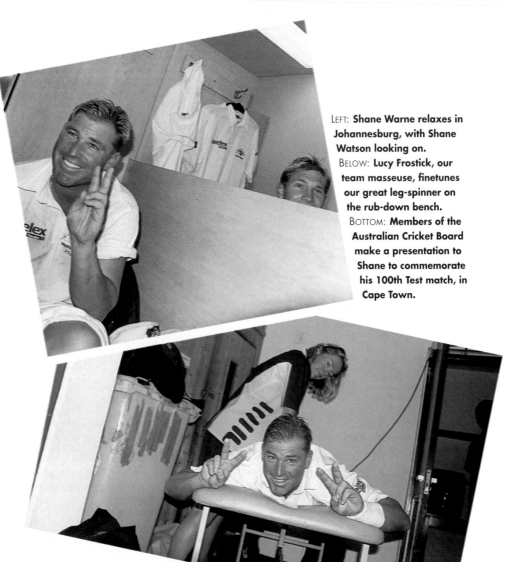

LEFT: **Shane Warne relaxes in Johannesburg, with Shane Watson looking on.**
BELOW: **Lucy Frostick, our team masseuse, finetunes our great leg-spinner on the rub-down bench.**
BOTTOM: **Members of the Australian Cricket Board make a presentation to Shane to commemorate his 100th Test match, in Cape Town.**

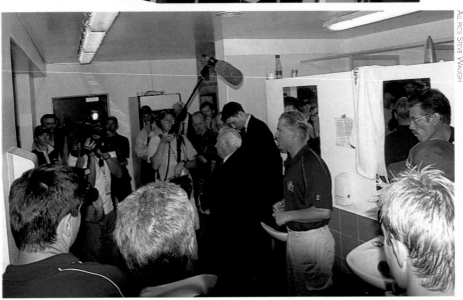

for a boundary, and an opportunity to drive at him appeared to materialise, but in my eagerness I missed a half-volley that, to the bowler's credit, was a quicker delivery than his previous one. There are few things worse than hearing the ball clang into the timber when you have not a single run to your name. It gives you a nauseous sensation in the pit of your stomach, and you wish time could be reversed just for that ball so you could make things right. I guess that's what makes this game such a great one; it can be so rewarding, yet terribly deflating, and always challenging. You can never take anything for granted and have to keep working at trying to improve your game. The moment you relax, the game takes control of you.

The excellent scoring rate we had achieved had again put us in a great position to win the game with over three days to go. We finished with a first-innings lead of 143, which could have been even better had we not left the field after a few overs with both Herschelle Gibbs and Gary Kirsten looking a little unsure. A crazy aspect of this end to the day's play was the fact that we went off for bad light even though the lights which are used for day/night games were on. Where is the logic in that?

A night in, watching *American Psycho* on my DVD player, did nothing to allow me a decent night's sleep, especially because the movie came on top of the 100 or so replays of today's batting failure that I reviewed in my mind.

March 10

Cape Town

South Africa v Australia, Second Test, Newlands, Cape Town
South Africa 239 and 4–307 (105 overs: HH Gibbs 39, G Kirsten 87, GC Smith 68, JH Kallis 73; SK Warne 3–100) v Australia 382

ANOTHER MISSED FAMILY BIRTHDAY WHILE on tour, but I'm sure by now that Mum accepts it as being the normal way to celebrate it.

Today turned out to be one of the toughest days of Test cricket of my career. It was over six and a half hours in the blazing sun, during which time we managed to secure four South African wickets as the pitch flattened out into a batting paradise. With only four specialist frontline bowlers, who by late afternoon were all suffering from fatigue, the Waugh brothers and Damien Martyn also rolled their arms over to give the specialists a chance to recuperate. Shane Warne was outstanding, with both his accuracy and endurance, and kept us in control of the match or at least on a level par. I was extremely proud of our efforts in the last session, keeping South Africa to only 87 runs from 37 overs, when we could have let the game slip away. It showed enormous courage and commitment to keep on going and hang in there.

Our departure from the ground was delayed a good half an hour to allow the police dog squad to scour over every inch of the bus in search of a possible bomb. This was necessary after a phone call was made to the ground saying that 'the Australian team will be eliminated tonight on the way home'. It was a 99 per cent chance that this was a hoax, but to be sure we were glad the one per cent option was considered. Touring life will often throw up these interruptions: during my time there have been, to my knowledge, more than half a dozen threats to our safety. After such a tiring day in the field, most of the lads stayed in for a spot of TV and room service — in preparation for tomorrow's crucial play that will decide the outcome of the Test.

March 11

Cape Town

South Africa v Australia, Second Test, Newlands, Cape Town
South Africa 239 and 473 (162 overs: ND McKenzie 99, MV Boucher 37; SK Warne 6–161) v Australia 382 and 1–131 (33 overs: JL Langer 58, ML Hayden 50 not out, RT Ponting 17 not out)

AS OFTEN HAPPENS, THE REWARDS come after the hard work, and in our case that hard work was put in yesterday. Warney turned in a colossal effort, sending down 98 overs for the match of which 70 came during our marathon 162 overs in the South African second innings. Without his stamina and consistency we would have struggled to bowl South Africa out today, but it was in fact two brilliant pieces of fielding that turned the match our way.

Often, when a batsman is nearing a milestone, he tends to tighten up, thinking about what he's going to achieve, which consequently leads to a loss of concentration and an opportunity for the bowlers or fieldsmen to prey on a half chance. That's exactly what occurred today, when the stalking Brett Lee pounced on a McKenzie on-drive — sliding on his knees and then throwing all in the one action — to catch a casual Andrew Hall a couple of centimetres short of his ground. Mind you, even with Binger's moment of magic there was still work to be done and Jason Gillespie at the bowler's end scooped up the throw on the half volley and broke the stumps to complete a quality team dismissal.

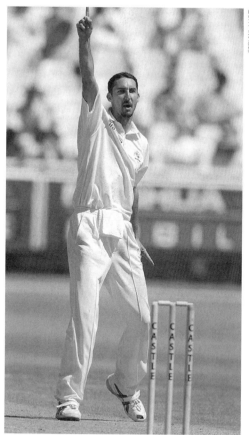

Jason Gillespie grabs the important wicket of South African captain Mark Boucher.

More was to follow, as the obsessively superstitious Neil McKenzie panicked on 99, taking off for a risky single in search of his hundred after he cracked one to Damien Martyn's left at cover. In a brilliant piece of athleticism, Marto gathered the ball in his non-throwing left hand, transferred the ball to his right hand, spun around on his knees and threw down the stumps at the bowler's end to shatter the timber and McKenzie's dreams of a hometown hundred. It was a senseless run out, but maybe not too surprising considering how worked up McKenzie gets himself with his routines and rituals. At the end of each over, he must walk past halfway down the pitch to meet the other batsman, then he turns and steps off the pitch, walks back to the batting end to re-enter near the stumps, and throughout is desperate not to touch any lines. His pre-delivery routine is extensive, as he scratches around the crease, adjusts his gear and looks in certain directions. When he's at the non-striker's end, he stands inside the return crease right next to the stumps. Being so careful not to do the wrong thing must be mentally taxing and has become something we are keen to exploit.

Brett Lee began these mind games as McKenzie entered the nervous 90s. 'Hey Macca,' Bing said. 'You just trod on a line, that's gonna cost you!' Whether he did or didn't tread on a line was irrelevant; that little voice in his head was now saying, 'Maybe I did, I hope it doesn't jinx me or cause me to get out.'

As I have said many times, in my opinion this is gamesmanship, not sledging. Too often, people confuse the two.

After South Africa had lost their sixth wicket of the day for 166, to be all out for 473, we required 331 to win — on what was still a batting paradise — to clinch the series. By stumps, we had whittled the target down to exactly 200, thanks to some ultra-aggressive and sometimes fortunate batting from our top three, who are all in dynamic touch at the moment.

A regular visitor to the change-rooms during this Test has been Merv Hughes, who is here as a tour group leader and escorts a heap of cricket-crazy supporters to our matches. While on tour, the 'big fella' has filled in and dabbled with the commentary team. To make this challenging the boys have been giving him words or phrases that he has to slip into his descriptions of play during the day. 'Peter Brady', from the famous *Brady Bunch* television series, seemed a particularly challenging one, or at least we thought so. Not for Merv. After fellow commentator Mike Haysman described Paul Adams as being unique in his bowling action, Merv nonchalantly replied, 'No, it's not unique. A guy called Peter Brady used to play second grade at my club and bowled exactly the same way.' A bewildered Haysman didn't know what to think, but Merv kept a straight face and continued commentating with nobody in his audience sensing they'd been had.

'Snuffalufagus', as in 'Mr Snuffalufagus', a character from *Sesame Street*, was a word that we thought would be impossible for him to use with any degree of sanity, but the challenge only lifted Merv to greater heights. After combining for another 100-run partnership, the now traditional Hayden/Langer midwicket show of affection was, in Merv's words, a real 'snuffalufagus'. There's nothing the lovable Victorian can't do and it's always terrific having him around, as his positive outlook is always uplifting to those he comes into contact with.

March 12

Cape Town

South Africa v Australia, Second Test, Newlands, Cape Town

South Africa 239 and 473 lost to Australia 382 and 6–334 (79.1 overs:
ML Hayden 96, RT Ponting 100 not out) by four wickets

A BRIEF CHAT BEFORE WARM-UPS from Buck and then a few words from myself gave the same message to everyone. Try to put the score and the end result out of our minds and just go out and play — follow the process and enjoy the day. Simple enough, but on most occasions thoughts about chasing a victory can be all-consuming and end up strangling your chances of success.

In the end we did succeed, after a day in which for a while it seemed we'd win relatively comfortably, then it seemed we might not triumph at all, and then we did get home, after one the more nervy spells of my career. A key moment, when the tension started to kick in, came when the backers of Matthew Hayden who took up the 12–1 odds offered by Centrebet on him matching The Don by scoring centuries in six Test matches in a row would have been kicking the TV in during the early hours back in Oz. When Matty chased a near wide off Jacques Kallis and Mark Boucher completed the job, 'Nature Boy' was just four runs short of what would have been hundred No. 5. His dismissal left us 2–201. When, 20 overs later, it was 5–268, the oddsmakers at Centrebet probably had things back around even money.

Fortunately for us, Ricky Ponting was playing one of his best knocks at this level, and he guided us home with the help of Adam Gilchrist (who again just came out and smashed 'em from ball one) and Shane Warne, who finished the job almost too well. I say almost too well because with three runs to win Ricky still needed a six to get his 10th Test-match hundred. Warney had belted 15 of their partnership of 23. Amazingly, though, Adams dragged down his stock delivery wrong 'un, and the Tasmanian pinned the ears back and completed the 'Cinderella story' in exactly the same manner we won the Second Test in Port Elizabeth five years ago. On that occasion, Ian Healy hit a six that broke the deadlock.

Pandemonium broke loose in the players' enclosure, at the realisation of our dream. A series win away from home and (if you combine the two

Matty Hayden looked destined for yet another Test-match hundred until he came unstuck when 96.

series against South Africa, home and away) a 5–0 lead against a team many thought could beat us. Only a player who's been in a change-room after such a win can explain the emotions that you experience — elation, joy, relief, satisfaction, camaraderie ... these are just a few of the words that spring to mind.

Everyone was so pleased for Ricky, reflecting another great aspect about this side. We are a group of blokes who genuinely enjoy each other's personal triumphs. There is a real happiness throughout the whole squad at what Punter achieved and what we have done for each other.

Our natural high as a team was somewhat short-lived, because here in Cape Town we actually have two dressing-rooms which are separated by a wall and have different entrances. I have never seen such a set-up anywhere else. It meant that we had to go back to our respective places to get our gear back in lockers and ourselves organised for the presentation, which detracted from the moment somewhat. After the presentation, we went on a lap of honour, a way to recognise and say thanks to our devoted and loyal fans who follow us around the world.

It was great for the guys with families to catch up and share the experience. I imagine for Warney, life doesn't get much better — a series win, being named man of the match in his 100th Test and having his family here to celebrate the moment with him. The boys from *60 Minutes* made it to the ground at precisely the time we needed three runs to win, and were keen to get some footage as we pressed the flesh with our supporters.

Back in the change-rooms, ACB Chairman Bob Merriman and Chief Executive James Sutherland took some time to discuss the upcoming Zimbabwe and Pakistan tours, stressing to us that they wouldn't be rushing into any decisions and would give top priority to our safety. Most of the guys were guarded in their comments, but a few expressed their anxiety. I must admit Zimbabwe sounds unstable and extremely volatile at the moment, while Pakistan may be even more of a worry after September 11 and our government's support of America. To some in Pakistan we are now seen as being part of the enemy. The name 'bin Laden' has cropped up in conversations between players during this tour, and while the war on terrorism goes on many of us will continue to hold fears that might be far-fetched, but might not be.

It was quite a while before I could find some time to savour the moment. As a captain, I have an overwhelming sense of pride in a great team accomplishment — a magnificent Test and series win. It's heartening to think that I have had an influence on what has happened; of course, each and everyone in the squad can feel exactly the same way. Scoring only 14 today was a downer, especially as every ball I received hit the middle of my bat except the one that got through my defence. I can handle getting bowled, but not when the manner of the out is almost identical to the way I was dismissed the previous time I went out to bat. Learning from mistakes is crucial to longevity and success, and I can't believe I fell victim the same way twice in the same match.

Just when we all thought our team celebratory song couldn't be bettered, up we went to Table Top Mountain, which offers a view as good as anywhere on earth. Making it even better, the cable car operator and owner of a bar at the peak was our host for the night. Long after the last tourist had departed, we gathered on a balcony, underneath the Southern Cross, which was set among a dazzling array of sparkling stars. This was a rare moment — like the team song on the pitch at Lords after the 1999 World Cup final — that we'll always remember from our time as a unit.

I doubt that we'll ever sing the team song from such an exotic location again. I doubt, too, that we'll ever be able to ride *outside* the cable car, held on by a harness, again — which we were able to do thanks to the generosity of the operator. Seeing Haydos, arms aloft with an Aussie flag draped across his back, leaning over the railing mimicking the scene from the movie *Titanic*, as we climbed back to the top, is a sight that will take some beating.

Capping my day off was the memory of some words from Stuart MacGill, who had taken time out to encourage and support me at the start of the day. It's always nice to be thought of, and his comments had a positive effect.

March 13

Cape Town to Durban

TOURING LIFE CAN BE SOMEWHAT difficult after an important Test win. The celebrations that follow can be brought to a shuddering halt when you remember that your bags have to be packed and ready by six the next

Modern international cricket throws up these kinds of images, as often the two teams find themselves travelling on the same plane, as the caravan moves from city to city. Here Shaun Pollock is just beating Shane Warne in the race to get from the luggage pick-up to the team buses.

morning and the team bus for the airport departs at 8.15. Invariably, anyone who misses the bus in such circumstances gets such a shock that he will get dressed in record time, hail a cab, and arrive at the airport before the team bus. That is exactly what happened here, but our 'sleepy head' — one of the quicks — didn't escape scot-free, as the team's 'ghetto blaster' is now in his possession for the next week.

The *60 Minutes* crew, led by presenter Peter Overton, was scheduled to do interviews and filming involving the team during the course of the day. Being captain meant I was required to do a longer interview, but I found it to be a positive 50 minutes, with the emphasis on the team aspect and what makes this Australian side such a great unit. Many of the team have been a little sceptical about the idea of the 'outside world' seeing what makes the team tick. I believe, like the rest of the boys, that to some degree scenes such as team meetings, dressing-rooms and private conversations should remain sacred and part of the fabric of the

Australian team and not be for wholesale consumption. Some have criticised my books for not going far enough in terms of 'behind the scenes' revelations, but there are good reasons for that which go even further than just simple privacy considerations. There has to be an element of mystique surrounding the team that keeps it one step ahead of the rest and unique to those who experience it.

A press conference involving the four Australian scribes on tour began with their usual 'half volley' (easy) questions until they progressed onto a barrage of bumpers (hard). The theme of the Waugh brothers failing took control and is clearly going to be the focus of tomorrow's headlines. My interrogation was curtailed by the need to join up with the lads for a walk along the beachfront to get the aches and pains out. A swim and a stretch rounded off the session, which was highlighted by Dizzy performing one of his favourite World Wrestling Federation headlocks on Peter Overton.

A small group of us ventured into the seedy part of Durban to catch the much-awaited film *Ali*, which was interesting but not as intoxicating as expected, although the 'slush puppies' and 'smarties' ensured that we were pretty well satisfied with the evening's entertainment.

March 14

Durban

TODAY IS PROBABLY THE BUSIEST day of the week for Lucy, as she attended to the needs of four batsmen and four bowlers in preparation for tomorrow's Test. Each massage takes an hour and is vital to the players' well-being, to get rid of those lurking little niggles in the muscles. Lucy has fitted into the team environment extremely well and is now a vital part of the squad's jigsaw. I've always been a big rap for the benefits of massage; to me it is both relaxing and therapeutic, and forms an integral part of my pre-match routine.

Another walk along the beachfront helped me gather my thoughts and spend some valuable time by myself, without media obligations or having to talk cricket to anyone. If I was to give Ricky Ponting any advice as a

It seems as if everything **Adam Gilchrist** touches on this tour turns to gold. He's even scoring the winning tries in touch footy matches — events which, of course, need to be wildly celebrated.

When to Retire?

The question came up again when I chatted today with the Aussie reporters — when am I going to call it a day? Part of me would like to spit out, 'When I'm good and ready!' but I understand, after my omission from the one-day squad, why the press are asking. The truth is that while I don't know exactly when, I do know that I'm far from ready to give it away now.

I would like to leave on a positive note, certainly under better circumstances than when I was dropped from the one-day team straight after we'd failed to reach the finals of the VB Series. I'd like to depart with the team on top and me doing well. I don't want to leave Test cricket by getting a tap on the shoulder from the selectors or with the side losing.

I can also assure everyone that money and statistics won't determine when I retire. I hope I'm going to retire when I feel I've achieved everything I want to, when I feel it's the right time. Whether I'll be lucky enough to have it work out this way, only time can tell.

If I'm trying to keep playing but I haven't got that competitive instinct, I'm sure a gut feeling will come in and say, 'Enough's enough.'

For now, I'm desperately keen to continue, despite the fact that I haven't been scoring as many runs lately as I would have liked. I believe that senior players are entitled to some slack, but not too much. I know Mark Taylor was given an extended run in 1996–97, more than 20 innings without a fifty at one stage, but I wouldn't expect to hold my spot in similar circumstances. But it's not as if I'm going through such a sequence. I averaged more than 50 with the bat through 2001, am still averaging 50 in Test cricket (though only just, I admit) and it's not so long ago that I was scoring a ninety against South Africa in a Test at the Melbourne Cricket Ground.

Go back to England just six months ago and I was hitting the ball as well as I've ever hit it. I came back from that tour and had six weeks off to get over the effects of DVT syndrome on my leg, circumstances that threw me out of kilter a bit. Today, I know I'm still good enough to go out there and score runs.

I just have to keep trusting myself.

captain, it would be to make sure he gives himself some time in his schedule for his own thoughts, so he can get away from all the hustle and bustle of life as an international cricketer.

Before training, it was again time to oblige the media with the host broadcaster, who wanted me to spend two minutes with cricket's coolest of interviewers, the former West Indian quick Michael Holding, who doesn't seem to be fazed by anything. The *60 Minutes* guys followed me into the general press conference, which was pretty tame compared with normal, except for one question. 'Is it true that the *60 Minutes* crew are here to film Mark and yourself announce your retirements together?' I was asked. Just another rumour in a season full of mistruths and speculation.

Training involved a combination of fitness and skill work, and lasted for around two and a half hours. Again, I feel in good shape and only need to get the basics right to score runs. Keep it simple, concentrate and trust myself. Without doubt, the roughest part about cricket — probably all big-time sport — is the negative thoughts that get inside your head. The 'little voice' can be very destructive and eat away at your confidence if you don't switch it off or use it to your advantage. The best way is to know you've done everything possible with your preparation and that every base has been covered. If you have done the hard work then you can ask no more of yourself. This is when you have to trust that it will work, as long as you combine that effort with on-field concentration.

This evening's team meeting was a waste of time, as our computer system seized up, much to Mike Walsh's dismay and frustration. It must have been galling for him, as he has worked hard to ensure its success. I must admit I was frustrated at its inability to work too, because it seemed to lead to an absence of attention from many of the squad. We must respect our opposition if we are to create our own history and win the home-and-away series 6–0. During the meeting, I thanked our four reserves, who have all been fantastic, and mentioned that if we didn't give this match our full attention and commitment then we'd be disrespecting the efforts of our 'benchies'.

It was fabulous to see Lynette arrive in town and instantly I felt more confident and relaxed about the upcoming match. Leaving three young kids behind is not easy and I certainly appreciate the sacrifice she has made to be here with me. As it is in most cases, your partner will often know what to say or how to say it just when it matters most. The partners of most of the players have been with us since the second Test and the whole operation and process of the girls travelling with us has once again been well received and beneficial to everyone. Times have changed. It was only back in 1997 that the wives and girlfriends were only allowed to stay in the team hotel for the last two weeks of a four-month Ashes tour. That is not an ideal situation and to me represented poor man-management from the people in charge.

March 15

Durban

South Africa v Australia, Third Test, Kingsmead, Durban

Australia 315 (74.1 overs: RT Ponting 89, ME Waugh 45, AC Gilchrist 91) v South Africa 1–48 (12 overs: HH Gibbs 24 not out)

Gilly kept his batting average for the series well over 200, and his scoring rate at better than a run a ball by making 91 from 107 balls on the opening day in Durban.

FOR THE THIRD TEST IN a row, I was quite happy to lose the toss. On one hand, the pitch had a good grass coverage, which would no doubt assist the quick bowlers, at least for the first session, if Mark Boucher decided to put us in. Countering this, we would also have the advantage of bowling last on a wicket that would no doubt be playing up and down and turning. My gut feeling was to bowl, but I was quite happy to let Boucher make the decision, and I was almost certain he would get us to bat.

To me, the benefits of winning the toss are as overrated as the alleged positives of getting a suntan, eating anchovies or doing aerobics. Anyway, the coin fell Boucher's way and we were sent in.

Immediately Justin Langer went after the bowling in cavalier fashion, which was the perfect way to send the opposition a message that we meant business. However, it came unstuck when he tried to give David Terbrugge the same treatment he'd handed out to the unlucky-to-be-dumped Dewald Pretorius in Cape Town. Lang went for a pull shot, but the resulting top edge was snapped up and the first battle was lost. However, the idea behind the shot was an admirable one.

The scoring rate was again exceptional, but our application and concentration weren't as commanding as usual.

All in all, being bowled out with 16 overs remaining in the day on a perfect batting pitch was a substandard effort. In my view

Ricky Ponting at Newlands, carrying on where he left off after his superb century in the second Test.

there is no doubt that our total of 315 is at least 150 short of what we should have ended up with.

Going out to bowl, we needed a breakthrough before stumps to end the day feeling on top or at least on level terms. The lack of natural light necessitated the floodlights being switched on, but even with the artificial help we eventually came off a little early, and with just the one scalp. But what a crucial one it could turn out to be, as Gary Kirsten gloved one down the leg-side off Binger during a short, sustained and hostile spell that had us cringing in the cordon at the possibility of a serious injury occurring. Brett would love to bowl this way all the time, but such is the effort and energy required that he risks causing himself a long-term injury, one that evolves over time, if he constantly lets himself go. Still, we should be thankful that he can produce this type of devastating spell on a reasonably regular basis.

Earlier, during our innings, I'd again left the ground with a failure next to my name and again it was Paul Adams who dismissed me. This game can be tormenting. My extended lack of success with the bat has become a real test of my nerves, durability, temperament and determination. I know a big score isn't far away, and I must keep the faith and continue to work hard in the nets. The results will come.

March 16

Durban

South Africa v Australia, Third Test, Kingsmead, Durban
Australia 315 and 8–159 (42 overs: RT Ponting 34, ME Waugh 30, SR Waugh 34 not out, B Lee 5 not out; JH Kallis 3–18) v South Africa 167 (55.2 overs: HH Gibbs 51; B Lee 4–82, SK Warne 4–33)

TODAY WAS ONE OF THE craziest days of Test cricket I've ever been involved in, with 17 wickets falling on one of the flattest pitches any batsman could ever dream about. It was either brilliant bowling or substandard batting, and I believe it was the latter.

Shane Warne batting on day one of the third Test. Warney's batting was something of a revelation throughout the 2001–02 season.

Ricky Ponting has just ended the second Test by hitting a six to reach his hundred, and isn't he happy about it!

There's no doubt Adam Gilchrist was the player of the series. ABOVE: Gilly is satisfied, if slightly on edge, as he comes into the dressing-room during the tea break on the second day of the first Test. At this moment he was 199 not out.
BELOW: The scene in the change-room immediately after another miraculous Gilchrist century, scored in the second Test. A feature was a 39-run last-wicket partnership with Glenn McGrath, of which Pigeon smashed 2.

Above: **Shane Warne, playing his 100th Test, is man of the match in Cape Town.**
Below: **Something we'll never grow tired of — acknowledging our fans after a totally satisfying triumph away from home.**

ABOVE: **Time to relax and celebrate. Mine is an Amarula and milk (which tastes like a caramel version of Baileys), while Lucy enjoys a beer and Jock sticks to soft drink.**
BELOW: **This is nowhere near as easy as it looks. Watto shows some of our fitness gurus how it's done.**

BOTH PICS STEVE WAUGH

ABOVE: **Lang and Haydos — a great combination on and off the field.**
BELOW: **Tour selector Allan Border shares a thought or two with Boof Lehmann** (LEFT) **and Dizzy Gillespie in Jo'burg.**

ABOVE: **Brett Lee (closest to camera), Justin Langer and the rest of the lads stretch tired muscles on the beachfront not long after we'd arrived in Durban to prepare for the third Test.**
BELOW: **As Watto looks on, Warney proves to the locals that his talents extend beyond spinning a leg break.**

Mark Waugh had a tour where many in the media wanted to tell him he was totally out of form. However, in reality, he didn't go too badly, never failing to reach double figures and averaging nearly 50 for the trip. ABOVE: **A typically elegant glide to the leg side during his century against South Africa A in Port Elizabeth.** BELOW: **Bowling on the third day of the third Test, when he took 2–26.**

My last Test innings in South Africa was a top-score 42. How I would have loved to turn it into a really big one.

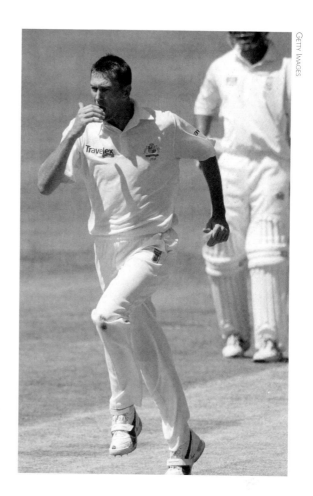

Glenn McGrath takes huge delight in dismissing Graeme Smith for 1 early on the second day of the third Test. Smith was arguably the find of the series for South Africa, mainly because of his combative, determined approach.

Why? A couple of reasons. One, playing back-to-back Test matches is physically demanding but mentally it's even more taxing. With batting at this level being such a mind game, the required arousal level and concentration focus can be lacking by the time of the second of the back-to-back games. And two, I feel that the fact that we have played so much cricket in such a short space of time against the same side also resulted in a drop-off in intensity, which led to a below-standard performance by both sides.

We were ecstatic after taking a 148-run lead, as we had expected South Africa to at least get close to our first-innings total. And personally I was really pleased with my captaincy, with every bowling change and field placement coming off. It's nice when it goes like that, because there are plenty of times I can't buy a trick. However, unbelievably, we then lost eight wickets for 159 in 42 overs before the close of play, due to careless strokeplay and some poor concentration. It was a real shame, especially as a score of even 250 in our second innings would virtually ensure that South Africa were out of the game. As it stands, they are now a 50–50 to win, because the pitch is still very placid in nature.

The difficult nature of our plight in this innings seemed to bring the best out in me and at the close I was 34 not out, but with only Brett Lee and Glenn McGrath to come. Our lead is now 307 and my hope is for another 40 or so runs tomorrow, so we can really put some question in their top order.

Lynette and I broke from our room-service routine, branching out for a feed of Japanese which was 10 classes above the soup and pasta of the day, and when I returned I found that a letter had been pushed under my door. It was a note that emphasised what a strong unit we are. Jock Campbell had dropped me a line, written in his unique style, that congratulated me on today's effort and urged more of the same for tomorrow. These seemingly small actions are what make up the 'X Factor', the thing that makes good sides great.

I drifted off to sleep imagining Binger and me putting on a big partnership ...

March 17

Durban

South Africa v Australia, Third Test, Kingsmead, Durban
Australia 315 and 186 (49 overs: SR Waugh 42; M Ntini 3–65, JH Kallis 3–29,) v South Africa 167 and 4–264 (84 overs: HH Gibbs 104, G Kirsten 64, GC Smith 42, JH Kallis 35 not out; ME Waugh 2–26)

IT WAS GOOD TO SEE the one-day boys at breakfast this morning and to finally meet Queensland's Nathan Hauritz for the first time. What a journey lies ahead for this 20-year-old, with a World Cup less than 12 months away. Jimmy Maher was his usual vibrant self, and it would be nice to see him do very well as he deserves success after working hard at his game. He strikes me as a player who has worked out his one-day strategy very well, who knows what and how he wants to play. I'm sure

Images from the third Test. TOP LEFT: **The idiosyncratic Neil McKenzie, who's a good player but probably too superstitious for his own good.** TOP RIGHT: **Left-arm spinner Paul Adams, who became something of a bogeyman for me during the final two matches of the series.** BOTTOM: **Mark Waugh square cuts on the first day, with the always excellent Mark Boucher behind the stumps.**

he'll do well. Bevo, of course, is a freak of a one-day batsman and Ian Harvey goes by that nickname, 'The Freak', at times as well. I wish them all the greatest of success.

At the Test, a day that promised so much delivered so little, much to our displeasure and surprise. It started promisingly enough, when Binger was dropped by new boy Terbrugge, an absolute sitter. But no such joy awaited me, when Jacques Kallis pulled out a phenomenal diving one-hander at second slip. It's amazing that things like this happen when 'things aren't going your way', but I've always believed that the wheel turns eventually.

When the home team went back in, the marathon effort of our bowlers in Cape Town definitely began to take its toll. We weren't very menacing or productive at all, and the fielding lacked intensity, as we waited for things to happen instead of making them occur. By stumps we were very much in the hot seat, requiring a further six wickets tomorrow for victory while the South Africans needed only 71 for a much-needed win.

Sitting in the rooms at the end of the day, it was hard to fathom how we had turned a first-innings lead of 149 into this perilous position in just a day and a half. Clearly, we had taken our foot off the accelerator and now we are paying the price. Test matches are hard work and never easy to win, contrary to reports of late. Today's play definitely reinforced this point. Perhaps some of our victories of late have been taken for granted, because we have achieved so much over the past couple of years.

March 18

Durban

South Africa v Australia, Third Test, Kingsmead, Durban
Australia 315 and 186 lost to South Africa 167 and 5–340 (104.5 overs:
JH Kallis 61 not out, AG Prince 48) by five wickets

THIS MORNING'S DILEMMA WAS THIS: who should I throw the ball to? We needed to get a quick breakthrough, to send the local dressing-room into a state of panic and give us a real chance of victory. Binger, to me, was the obvious choice, especially as we had only just taken the new ball —

and Brett bowled quick with it last night, and swung it as well. The other end was a toss-up between McGrath's consistency and Warney's variation. Tilting the balance in Pigeon's favour was the extra bounce and sideways movement off the seam that he may get.

The game plan was to keep Kallis tied down and restrict his boundaries by giving the bowlers protection in his key hitting areas. At the other end, we intended to attack the inexperienced Ashwell Prince and hopefully make him crack under the pressure. It sounded fair enough in the change-rooms, but obviously the South Africans also had a game plan and theirs won out as they beat us for the loss of only one more wicket. It was a deflating way to end the series.

One thing I can never understand is why you don't get the trophy for winning a series when you actually wrap up that series. Instead, it's always handed over after the final Test of the series. In my view, our amazing victory in Cape Town should have coincided with the handing over of the trophy, but the moment was lost and now certainly didn't feel like the appropriate time. Adam Gilchrist rightly walked away with the Man of the Series award, capping three matches in which he hit 473 runs

at an average of 157.67 and a run-rate of better than a run a ball and completed 14 dismissals behind the stumps.

By the time I finished my media commitments the lads had all but packed up and were quietly applying ice packs or having a beer. It was a strange way to end a fantastic series for us; our emptiness emphasised that winning is why we play the game.

Maybe our smiles would have been bigger if we'd received the trophies straight after we won the series in Cape Town. But even so we knew our triumphs in Australia and then here had cemented our rating as the No. 1 Test team in the world, so it wasn't too hard to grin when the photographers asked us to.

A team signing session followed by Buck's little tour awards and a tribute video on Mark and me was a nice way to round off the past five weeks we've enjoyed together as a team. A BBQ officially ended the Test match part of the tour, as the boys and their partners enjoyed a relaxed evening. It was good to have an extended chat to Punter about the captaincy, a task that I'm sure he'll handle very well. My main advice was to be your own man, make time for yourself and always back your gut instinct. Sidling up to Ricky and me was new boy Watto, who was inquisitive and impressive in his quest for improvement and knowledge. He certainly knows what he wants and that's an important start. Typical of Gilly, he wanted a few quiet words as to how he could be the vice-captain that Punter needs and wants. Basically I told him to do exactly what's he's doing now: monitor the mood and feeling of the side, show leadership qualities and be loyal to the captain.

It was a weird sensation, after bidding farewell to everyone, to walk away. It was almost like saying goodbye to your family. I guess the bonus is that Lynette and I are off on a two-day safari, while the boys will be on a plane and then straight to the nets tomorrow. Life goes on and I'm sure the sun will come up in the morning.

A Magical Place

With the third Test not going the full five days, and our flight home being rescheduled, Lynette and I took the chance to spend two days visiting the famed Sun City resort and the adjoining wildlife sanctuary park, Pilansberg. While it is very strange to be disassociated from the touring party, it hasn't been hard to relax at this man-made wonder located in the middle of nowhere. With wave pools, entertainment areas, first-class restaurants and casinos, topped off by superb accommodation, it is truly a magical place.

Even allowing for this out-of-this-world experience, we were both mesmerised by the beauty of the landscape and the majesty of seeing wild animals in their own environment, right next door to the resort. There's something special about spotting camouflaged beasts such as a herd of elephants or a couple of rhinos as they appear out of their feeding grounds. The immense stature and pure physical presence of all the animals is mind-blowing. How anyone would want to hunt any animal to extinction is beyond comprehension.

Without doubt, the highlight of our stay was the opportunity to be involved in the capture of a young male lion, in order to attach a new innovation in the study and care of lions by way of a GPS transmitter collar. These were seven of the best hours of my life. First, we tracked two males but then we incurred a flat tyre which needed to be changed with the two animals just 10 metres away. As the tyre was replaced, Gus, the team leader, focused on the lions with a rifle, just in case they wanted an extra feed, while all our hearts were nearly jumping out of our chests with fear. The fact that he has never had to kill an animal in this situation didn't seem to comfort us, but eventually we moved on to locate and track a pride of nine that was being sought.

In order to entice the lions a fresh kill of warthog was hung from a tree, while the warthog's intestines were dragged through the bushes. Further enticement came in the form of a recording of some pigs in their death cries. Sure enough, the lions came from everywhere, as did a number of safari tour groups, all keen for a look at what was happening. One of these developed a flat battery, which our driver fixed up while eight or nine lions roamed around in the darkness of night not far away. Eventually, a young male was darted, picked up after a seven-minute wait for the drugs to take effect, and then transported a few kilometres away to relative safety. Inspecting a lion at close quarters gave us a sense of its power and beauty. To be able to touch it and examine it will always be a treasured memory, and further guarantees my love affair with nature.

A hot air balloon safari topped off a wonderful two days. Then reality set back in and it was back to Jo'burg, before embarking on our trip back home. I know that when I hit home soil I will be on the end of another stern examination of my patience, as all sorts of stories about my future in the game will be on the boil. Already, an English paper has run a story that I am to be sacked from the Test side. It doesn't rain, it pours; but I have been told that this is all good for my character.

Which I guess it is!

PART 4

A CRICKETING 'OSCAR'

Two Australian cricketers with one of golf's greatest-ever players — Warney and me with South Africa's legendary Gary Player at the Monte Carlo Golf Club.

May 15

Monte Carlo

BEING NOMINATED FOR THE LAUREUS World Sports Awards was a tremendous honour for the Australian cricket team, made even more meritorious by the fact that we'd also been up for the team award in each of the previous two years. This means that we are the only sports team in the world to be nominated on all three occasions for these so-called Oscars of sport.

Fortunately for Shane Warne, Ricky Ponting, Glenn McGrath and me, the invitation to attend this fantastic event was also extended to our partners. (Mind you, the money we saved on the complimentary air travel was certainly more than made up for by the girls, who wanted to feel a part of the glitz and glamour of Monte Carlo and consequently needed to update their wardrobes for the occasion.) Upon landing in Nice, in the very south of France near the border with Monaco, after a 30-hour journey, we quickly realised that this was a different world we had been transported into. Brand-new Mercedes Benz cars were on hand to transport us to our hotels — which turned out to be only 20 minutes away thanks to our chauffeur, who cruised at 160 kilometres per hour in a 70k zone, with no obvious need or desire to slow down, for the entire journey. The luxurious waterfront accommodation was also paid for by our generous hosts, which we decided was particularly handy after we discovered that a bowl of fish soup in the hotel restaurant sets you back the equivalent of 48 Australian dollars.

The first activity on our agenda was a golf day at the prestigious Monte Carlo Golf Club, high up on

Everywhere we looked, there was another famous face.
TOP: **Morgan Freeman and Catherine Zeta-Jones.**
MIDDLE: **Formula 1's Juan Pablo Montoya, who was named the 'Newcomer of the Year'.**
BOTTOM: **Michael Johnson, hero of the Atlanta and Sydney Olympics, who in March had been elected to the World Sports Academy.**

TOP: **Two famous Scots — Motor racing's David Coulthard and the one and only Sean Connery.** MIDDLE: **Five-time winner of the Tour de France and Olympic Gold medallist Miguel Indurain.** BOTTOM: **Boris Becker, who won the Australian Open men's singles in 1996 and I think had some success at Wimbledon as well.**

the mountain ranges that surround this tiny principality. So high up, in fact, that we had to play the first five holes in a thick fog, where visibility at times was restricted to only 10 metres. For me, playing golf is generally a very 'social' thing, not to be taken seriously, and having played only twice in about the past four years, my heart was beating a little nervously as I made my way to the first tee. I was already shaking with nerves after meeting Sean Connery and Boris Becker on the practice fairway. Meeting the screen legend was an especially great thrill — his demeanour, manner and cheerful attitude to everyone he met only enhanced his status in my eyes.

I was teamed up with Warney, and pitted against two South Africans — one of whom, Johann Rupert, actually owns the concept of the Laureus Awards (as well as such notable brands as Dunhill, Cartier, Rothmans and Montblanc International, to name just a few of his assets). His partner was rugby legend Morné du Plessis, who is one of the members of the World Sports Academy.

When we arrived at the first tee I was astonished and dismayed to see a posse of camera crews waiting and keen to capture the moment. Sadly, my first shot was not a screamer down the middle, but an inside edge that bobbled embarrassingly into the nearby scrub. It was one of those moments you simply wish hadn't happened and I turned around to see everyone else looking in any direction but mine, pretending that it hadn't actually occurred.

From bad to worse is a fair description of my early 'progress', with the camera crews playing a significant role in the debacle that beset my second hole. Being in reasonably good shape for my third shot at a par four, not too far from the green, I went looking for a sand wedge, only to discover that there was no such implement in my hired set of clubs. I would have to rely on a bit of finesse from a

This shot looks better from this angle than if you were standing behind the sign, watching my ball disappear off the fairway.

pitching wedge to complete this delicate little shot. As luck would have it, a thick all-consuming fog then swept like a bullet across the fairway, just as I took my last deep breath before playing the shot. So now I was forced to play from memory. When the club made contact it actually felt pretty sweet — too sweet, in fact, to the point that I quickly realised it was destined for the car park, maybe the club house, whatever was located far beyond the green. Then I heard the sound of ball hitting something very solid, and I knew its progress had been abruptly halted.

What a stroke of good fortune, I thought to myself. I started picturing the ball on the green, after a miraculous ricochet, but as the fog cleared I saw it was sitting at the foot of a large tree adjacent to the green. Clearly, it seemed, that huge piece of timber had come to my aid. To the

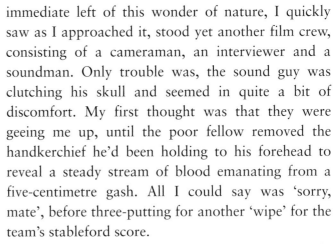

Above: **Who better to auction an hour's tennis with John McEnroe than the legend himself.**
Left: **The famous skier, Alberto Tomba.**
Below: **French tennis star Henri Leconte.**

immediate left of this wonder of nature, I quickly saw as I approached it, stood yet another film crew, consisting of a cameraman, an interviewer and a soundman. Only trouble was, the sound guy was clutching his skull and seemed in quite a bit of discomfort. My first thought was that they were geeing me up, until the poor fellow removed the handkerchief he'd been holding to his forehead to reveal a steady stream of blood emanating from a five-centimetre gash. All I could say was 'sorry, mate', before three-putting for another 'wipe' for the team's stableford score.

Incredibly, I ended up on the winning side, largely due to Shane's excellent performance and my occasional input. But even with the win, undoubtedly the highlight of our experience was Gary Player demonstrating the correct grip on the club with his knife at the lunch table before he tucked into his feed. My grip, predictably, is ideal for a cricket bat, but a long way from the one the great South African recommends for golf, where both hands should form a vee that points towards the back shoulder.

From golf we were whisked away to a media conference, which featured some of the all-time legends of sport. Sitting in the row in front of us were such notables as Mark Spitz, Franz Klammer, Nadia Comaneci, Michael Johnson, Edwin Moses and Ilie Nastase. In our row were 'Marvelous' Marvin Hagler, Dawn Fraser, Sir Bobby Charlton and many more stars. I didn't really feel comfortable being in such elite company, but I wasn't as intimidated as the world's media, who between them all didn't ask a single question until being prompted once again a good five minutes after initially being asked.

A dinner to raise funds for the 'Sport for Good' program, which is the main reason for this entire World Sports concept, went reasonably well except for a long delay caused by the late arrival of Prince Albert of Monaco. Among the items auctioned during the evening was a signed portrait of Boris Becker, which went for the equivalent of A$70,000, while an hour of tennis against John McEnroe went for A$30,000. That, to me, was a bargain.

The actual awards presentation was a spectacular affair, with movie stars such as Catherine Zeta-Jones, Michael Douglas, Morgan Freeman and Sean Connery giving the event a touch of glamour. Ten gold medallists from the recent Winter Olympics added to the prestige, while most of the 43 World Sports Academy members were in attendance. Sitting in my chair, waiting for the Team of the Year to be announced, I had a steady rotation of ailments — sweaty palms, stomach cramps, headache and droplets forming on the forehead. In my mind, I

ALL PICS GETTY IMAGES

TOP: **Sir Bobby Charlton, formerly of Manchester United and England.**
MIDDLE: **Marcel Desailly, now of Chelsea, and in 1998 a member of France's World Cup-winning side.**
BOTTOM: **Michael Jordan in full stride, with the ever-present bodyguard as his shadow.**

TOP: **One of our golfing partners, South African rugby legend Morné du Plessis.**
MIDDLE: **Kapil Dev with his wife and daughter. The great all-rounder is one of three cricketers in the World Sports Academy.**
BOTTOM: **Swimming immortal Mark Spitz, winner of seven gold medals at the Munich Olympics.**

went through an acceptance speech, just in case the late mail was right and we did happen to win. Adding to my anxiety was the fact that the ceremony was being telecast live to 180 countries, and being seen by an estimated audience of one billion people. That's a lot of people to see you fluff a speech.

The moment I saw Ian Botham — another World Sports Academy member — walking onto the stage to announce the team award winner I knew that we'd won. Now my stomach was really churning over, but at the same time I was elated and overwhelmed by the achievement. It was all over in a flash — my speech neither brilliant nor embarrassing — and then we were in a media enclosure talking to the press. And, unfortunately, what a fiasco the first two interviews turned into. The first came from an Indian crew, who asked three of the dopiest questions ever put, and all to Glenn McGrath. It seemed the interviewer had forgotten the rest of us were there. The second probe came from some Italians, whose interviewer clearly knew nothing about cricket and who asked his questions first in Italian and then in some very shaky English. The end result was hardly enlightening. And to finish off, he asked for a song! From us, one of the sporting world's most musically inept quartets! The right thing to do, I'm sure, was to just say no, sorry, but instead the first thing that came into my mind was our team song, 'Under the Southern Cross'. Halfway through the first or second line, I remembered how the song finished, and promptly panicked, blurting out a replacement word a line too early. Which killed the performance and left me looking at three startled teammates, who clearly thought I'd lost my marbles. I'm sure we came over a treat on Italian television and ensured that no young footballer from that country will be taking up cricket, at least in the near future.

ABOVE: **Players and partners on the streets of Monte Carlo.** FROM LEFT: **Shane and Simone Warne, Glenn and Jane McGrath, Lynette and Steve Waugh, Rianna Cantor and Ricky Ponting. Rianna and Ricky were married six weeks later.**
BELOW: **Reporters, microphones, cameras and spotlights crowd in on Catherine Zeta-Jones and Michael Douglas as they arrive at the Sport for Good Foundation dinner.**

ABOVE: **A photo opportunity before we headed to the first tee.** FROM LEFT: **Johann Rupert, Sean Connery, Morné du Plessis, Gary Player, Ian Botham, Boris Becker, Shane Warne and me.**
BELOW: **To be in the company of so many elite members of the World Sports Academy, including Australia's very own Mick Doohan and Dawn Fraser** (FAR LEFT)**, was a somewhat surreal experience.**

ABOVE: **If two cricketers of the modern era are suited to the glitz and glamour it's this pair: Warney and Ian Botham.**
RIGHT: **Footballer turned movie star Vinnie Jones amid the fog and mist at the Monte Carlo Golf Club.**

ABOVE: **Jennifer Capriati receives her Sportswoman of the Year statuette in Rome — where she was competing in the Tennis Masters Series event — from tennis legend and World Sports Academy member Martina Navratilova.**

LEFT: **With Shane Warne, Glenn McGrath, Ricky Ponting and the Team of the Year award.**

ABOVE: **Michael Schumacher, Sportsman of the Year after dominating Formula One throughout 2001.**
BELOW: **Goran Ivanisevic, whose victory over Pat Rafter at Wimbledon earned him the Comeback of the Year title.**

ABOVE: **The legendary gymnast Nadia Comaneci, who with track star Marion Jones and actor Dougray Scott hosted the Sportswoman of the Year presentation.**
BELOW: **Dutch wheelchair tennis champion Esther Vergeer.**

ABOVE: **Former US Masters and British Open champion Seve Ballesteros.**

RIGHT: **Glenn McGrath accepts the prize for hitting the longest drive at the golf.**

BELOW: **Kapil Dev** (LEFT) **and Boris Becker** (RIGHT) **take to the fairways.**

ABOVE: **John McEnroe (complete with New York Yankees cap) and Prince Albert at the celebrity tennis tournament.**
BELOW: **Marion Jones enjoys the rallies.**

ABOVE: **The Sport for Good Foundation dinner, held at the Salles des Etoiles in the Sporting Club in Monte Carlo the night before the awards ceremony, was quite an occasion.**
BELOW: **Members of the World Sports Academy on stage as Sean Connery prepares to present the Lifetime Achievement and the Sport for Good awards to Lady Pippa Blake, the widow of New Zealand yachting legend, Sir Peter Blake.**

It was only after we'd completed another 45 minutes of interviews and I had a chance to think about what we'd just won that it began to sink in — we'd been voted the best team on the planet! Considering that only a handful of the judges (the members of the World Sports Academy) would have anything but a vague notion of what cricket is all about, this must be a major breakthrough for the sport. Cricket needs to be a world game to maximise its potential and truly prosper in the increasingly competitive business that is world sport in the 21st century, and perhaps this recognition will prove to be a catalyst for some serious growth for the sport.

An after-function party for the invitees and many prominent local identities, conducted at the outrageously expensive 'Jimmy's' nightclub — how does A$35 for a coke sound? — capped off a wonderful two days. The prices didn't seem to bother anyone, even if they were more than a tad heavy for me. Catching up with five-time world champion motorcyclist Mick Doohan was a highlight, as was being introduced to Miguel Indurain, the five-time winner of the Tour de France. The only downer for the night was being shoved aside by one of Michael Jordan's bodyguards. My wife Lynette and I were minding our own business when a tidal wave of massive bodies came charging towards us. Forming a circle around this sporting legend were five enormous men who were hell bent on not letting anyone near their man, so much so that it seemed — in their eyes, at least — that anything in their vicinity was fair game. I must admit the incident left a sour taste in my mouth. Maybe there was a reason for their behaviour — perhaps in the US it has to be that way — but it didn't seem warranted here.

At around 3am we decided we'd spotted enough stars and chatted to enough celebrities, so we called it a night. What an extraordinary couple of days it has been, one we'll never forget.

TOP: **The former middleweight champion Marvelous Marvin Hagler.**
MIDDLE: **Kip Keino, first of the great Kenyan middle-distance runners.**
BOTTOM: **Another legendary track champion, Edwin Moses, now chairman of the World Sports Academy.**

The Laureus World Sports Awards

The annual Laureus World Sports Awards is the only awards ceremony staged to honour the best sportsmen and women in the world for their achievements across all disciplines. The 2002 event was the third time the Awards have been conducted.

There is a two-part selection process for determining the winners. First, a selection panel — made up of some of the world's leading sports journalists from over 75 countries — nominate five individuals (or teams) for each category. Then, the top five nominations are put to the members of the 'Laureus World Sports Academy', who choose the winners.

There are seven categories: Sportsman of the Year, Sportswoman of the Year, Team of the Year, Newcomer of the Year, Comeback of the Year, Alternative Sportsperson of the Year and Sportsperson of the Year with a Disability. In addition, two other awards are presented — a 'Lifetime Achievement' Award and a 'Sport for Good' Award. The latter is given to

This mightn't have been the finest speech I ever made, but it was certainly one of the proudest.

Monaco royalty meets sports royalty — Michael Jordan with Prince Albert.

an individual who has made an outstanding contribution to society through sport.

The Academy is chaired by 400-metre track hurdles legend Edwin Moses, and consists of 44 former elite athletes who have made an outstanding contribution to world sport (the election of the 44th member, the four-times Olympic Gold medallist in table tennis, Deng Yaping of China, was announced on May 14). The full list of Academy members is: Giacomo Agostini, Seve Ballesteros, Franz Beckenbauer, Boris Becker, Ian Botham, Sergei Bubka, Sir Bobby Charlton, Sebastian Coe, Nadia Comaneci, Morné du Plessis, Emerson Fittipaldi, Sean Fitzpatrick, Dawn Fraser, Tanni Grey-Thompson, Miguel Indurain, Jackie Joyner-Kersee, Michael Johnson, Michael Jordan, Kapil Dev, Kip Keino, Franz Klammer, Niki Lauda, Greg LeMond, Ivan Lendl, Sugar Ray Leonard, Dan Marino, Edwin Moses, Nawal el Moutawakel, Robby Naish, Ilie Nastase, Martina Navratilova, Jack Nicklaus, Pelé, Michel Platini, Gary Player, Hugo Porta, Sir Vivian Richards, Bill Shoemaker, Mark Spitz, Daley Thompson, Alberto Tomba, Katarina Witt, Yasuhiro Yamashita and Deng Yaping.

Athletes can only be elected to the Academy after their sporting careers have concluded. An exception to that rule was made for the

British wheelchair athlete Tanni Grey-Thompson, who was elected in 2001 'in a mark of respect for the extraordinary contribution she has made to her sport and to the world in general'.

The winners announced at the 2002 ceremony were as follows:

Sportsman of the Year: Michael Schumacher (motor racing)
Sportswoman of the Year: Jennifer Capriati (tennis)
Team of the Year: Australian cricket team
Newcomer of the Year: Juan Pablo Montoya (motor racing)
Comeback of the Year: Goran Ivanisevic (tennis)
Alternative Sportsperson of the Year: Bob Burnquist (skateboarding)
Sportsperson of the Year with a Disability: Esther Vergeer
    (wheelchair tennis)
Lifetime Achievement Award: Sir Peter Blake (yachting)
Sport for Good Award: Sir Peter Blake (yachting)

The nominees for the major awards were as follows:

Sportsman of the Year: Lance Armstrong (cycling), Maurice
    Greene (track and field), Michael Schumacher (motor racing),
    Ian Thorpe (swimming) and Tiger Woods (golf).
Sportswoman of the Year: Jennifer Capriati (tennis).
    Inge de Bruijn (swimming), Stacy Dragila (track and field),
    Annika Sorenstam (golf) and Venus Williams (tennis).
Team of the Year: Australian cricket team, Bayern Munich football
    club, Ferrari's Formula One motor racing team, French Davis
    Cup tennis team, Los Angeles Lakers basketball team.

The previous winners of the Sportsmen of the Year, Sportswomen of the Year and Team of the Year were:

2001: Tiger Woods, Cathy Freeman and the French men's football team.
2000: Tiger Woods, Marion Jones and Manchester United.

One interesting fact is that an Australian individual or team has been honoured in each of the three years. Not only did we win the Team Award in 2002, and Cathy Freeman the Sportswoman of the Year in 2001, but in 2000 the amazing Louise Sauvage was named the Sportsperson of the Year with a Disability.

PART 5

A QUICK LOOK
AT THE POMS

I signed a number of autographs during my 'off season', in places as far apart as Kolkata in India, Sydney, Australia, and here, in mid-August, at Canterbury in England.

August 31

Canterbury

IF YOU HAD TOLD ME 12 months ago, when I arrived back in Australia after a successful Ashes campaign, how the first nine months of 2002 would actually pan out for me, I would never have believed you. If you had said that I would not play a competitive match between mid-March and mid-August I would have laughed and reminded you that this was 2002 not 1972, and that these days the international cricket calendar is clogged solid. But now, of course, in the short term at least, my cricket life has changed.

While Ricky Ponting's team was comprehensively whacking South Africa 5–1 in the one-dayers that followed the South African Tests (the '1' being the last game of the series), I was either at home watching on television or on a short but very enjoyable holiday with my family. As the Australians were preparing for another one-day series, against Pakistan in Melbourne (two games indoors) and Brisbane in early June, I found myself in Chennai in India, doing some promotional work for MRF, my bat sponsor, including spending time at a Dennis Lillee-led MRF Foundation coaching camp. Three weeks later I was back on the subcontinent, this time in Kolkata and Chennai.

In Kolkata, I was keen to visit Udayan — the home for the daughters of leprosy sufferers in Barrackpore that I have supported as patron since 1998 — and see for myself the progress that has been made on the special projects that I have been involved in. As well, I was hoping my visit would help garner some corporate support for further projects of a similar vein to Udayan, and also, more generally, bring a greater awareness and understanding of the disease. It's not easy to find that corporate support, because there are so many deserving and needy causes, but though it might not be easy, I think we have an obligation to help people who are less fortunate than ourselves. I know I've been very lucky in my life, and there's only so much money that you can use and need. Why not help other people?

We didn't arrive at Udayan until around 2.30 in the afternoon of the only full day I had in Kolkata, to be told that the children had been waiting patiently in orderly queues since noon. For the previous few hours I had been shown a number of potential sites for a second girls' home, along similar lines to the first, but I don't think we were late, more that everyone was just eager to greet us. We were met with garlands and flower petals, and shouts of 'Steve Uncle!!', as they all tried to get my attention at once. In all, I spent around two-and-a-half fantastic and absorbing hours there, including some quiet times with nine-year-old Lakhi Kumari, who I am personally sponsoring.

In many ways, getting involved with the Udayan concept changed my attitude to life. I always wanted the girls here to enjoy the same opportunity as the sons of leprosy sufferers, who had had a rehabilitation centre built for them a few years earlier. I'm lucky; the steps that led to me being involved all fell into place. Sometimes in life you go in a direction without knowing why.

In Chennai for the second time in three weeks, I appeared at some functions and a product launch in my role as a brand ambassador for the new insurance company AMP–Sanmar. This joint venture, between the Chennai-based Sanmar group that specialises in engineering, shipping and specialty chemicals and the Australian insurance company AMP, was established at the start of 2002 and I was invited to become a brand ambassador soon after.

At the launch I was introduced to the throng and offered a few words of endorsement for a new Group Term Assurance policy, after which the company heads got down to the serious business of explaining what they were about. Then it was time for me to sign a few autographs and talk to the invited guests. I enjoyed watching apparently hard-nosed journalists, who had just been pressing the boss of AMP–Sanmar with uncompromising enquiries about budgets and marketing plans, suddenly become starstruck fans when the time for tricky questions ended and the time for photographs and signatures began. In no time, I was surrounded by not only reporters but also security guards, hotel waiters and many other non-business types who'd snuck into the function in various guises. 'I don't think I'll ever get used to that,' I said to the correspondent from the website *cricinfo* when I was asked afterwards about this acclaim, which is not directed purely at me but at all high-profile cricketers. 'You might do if you lived here, but living in Australia and coming to India only sporadically, it amazes me more and more every time. It's pretty incredible the following cricket has in India. In fact, it's actually good to go back to Australia, get your feet back on the ground, and realise that you're a normal human being, just like everyone else.'

I was overwhelmed by the greeting I received when I arrived at Udayan.

Wherever I went, I was truly astonished by the size and enthusiasm of the crowd that greeted me. In Kolkata I'd needed security to push through the multitude of people, photographers and TV crews at the airport early in the afternoon. Even in the city lanes on the way to the hotel there were a good many supporters. One thing that confused me was the crowd was yelling out for 'Waughda' and 'Steveda'. It took me a while to realise that it was actually me they were acknowledging.

But whenever I did a media interview, the first thing the reporters always wanted to know was how I was feeling about being left out of the one-day squad. At the airport the first question went this way: 'Has the Australian middle order been weakened by your's and Mark Waugh's absence?' 'I can't say that they have a bad combination,' I replied, 'just because myself and Mark are out of the side. But I'm waiting for my chance.'

Second question: 'Do you want to play one-day cricket for Australia?'

'I am very ambitious about returning to the one-day side.'

The smiles on the faces of the children is one thing that will always keep me coming back.

'How do you think India will go in the World Cup?' was question number three.

'I don't think they're among the favourites. Australia have the finest of teams. South Africa, being the hosts, will be tough to beat, while Pakistan are a well-balanced team. India are a good one-day team, but they might struggle on the bouncy wickets in South Africa. But the World Cup is still a long way away and any one of half a dozen sides can win it, including India.'

I must have deflected those first two questions pretty well. 'India not hot for Cup: Steve' was the next morning's headline on the main *Times of India* sports page.

At the AMP–Sanmar launch I was asked what gave me the greater pleasure, winning a Test (actually, it was 'winning a Test against India') or charity work. The truth, I explained — making sure I worded my answer exactly right — is that I get pleasure out of both. Winning a Test match is difficult, satisfying and enjoyable, sometimes gloriously so. But seeing the kids at Udayan happy and growing up under the care of people who have put in so much hard work — that, too, is immensely satisfying, if in a different way. I just feel delighted to be involved with the work.

I was also asked whether the fact I was here doing charity work was some sort of precursor to my retirement. 'I cannot concentrate on cricket because there is no cricket at the moment,' I explained. In fact, there is a time for both. Cricket remains my profession, hopefully for a while yet. And I also have my family, to whom I want to devote as much time as I can.

At the cricket camp I'd said that 'I cannot do anything about things that are not in my control. My philosophy is simple: give 100 per cent to my comeback bid.' One thing I have had reaffirmed many times over the past few months is that just like life there are no guarantees in cricket.

Whether or not you succeed in big-time sport, in most things really, depends to a large degree on how competitive you are; it is about desire. When someone brought up the subject of my age — I don't think there's a cricket writer in the world who doesn't know I was born on 2 June 1965 — I pointed to the example of Alec Stewart in England, who has been recalled to the national team at age 39 and is once again doing extremely well. Cricket is about opportunities and making the best of them. You can only lead a player to a certain point — something coaching clinics such as this one are very good at — but thereafter he has to back himself. That is a point I emphasised at the camp when talking to the opening bat, Sadagopan Ramesh, who played against us in 2001 and is hoping to re-establish himself in the Indian Test XI. I was able to cite Matthew Hayden as the perfect example of how important a never-say-die spirit is if you want to achieve your cricket goals.

Back home in Australia, a couple of interesting cricket matters caught my eye. One was the decision by the ICC to trial giving the third umpire a say in lbw decisions (the plan was to do this during the ICC Trophy tournament in September), the other the question of whether we're playing too much international cricket these days. On the former, frankly I couldn't believe that the ICC had gone this far with the video ump. In my view, the game is getting too 'Americanised', with too much technology coming into it. One of the reasons cricket is such a wonderful game is that it generates so much debate, fans can discuss rulings and speculate what might have been. Take that away and you lose much of the beauty and uniqueness of cricket. And anyway, in the main, I reckon the top umpires these days are doing a good job. There's no doubt in my mind that over the course of my career the standard of umpiring across the world — at the highest level at least — has improved significantly.

As to the amount of cricket we're playing, I'm pretty pragmatic. There's an enormous amount of money involved in the game these days, and the top players who are making a dollar have a responsibility to play. I think 12 to 14 Tests and 25 to 30 one-day internationals per year is a reasonable ask. Maybe this packed schedule will lead to more players opting to appear in just one form of the game rather than both, as Jonty Rhodes has done. Maybe some fast bowlers will have to do this if they want to prolong their careers. I would like to play both Tests and one-dayers, but it's an individual's decision.

Initially, it had seemed my chances of getting back into the Australian one-day side had taken another blow in mid-July when I'd been left out of an Australia A one-day team that was chosen for a September tour of South Africa. The selectors picked quite a few young guys for the A side, but also took the time to explain to me that they were aware of what Mark and I can do and wanted to observe some other players at close quarters. So being left out was not necessarily a negative thing.

All I can do — in regard to my cricket future — is give my total best whenever I play, whether it be for Australia in Test matches or for NSW in the Pura Cup and ING Cup (our domestic one-day competition). The coming season is an important one for me, but I don't want to put too much pressure on myself. If I focus too much on getting back into the one-day team, I might lose track of what I need to do to succeed. I have always tried to forget everything else and just concentrate on playing the next ball to the best of my ability. That's the way I want to approach the rest of my career. There were maybe one or two things that I needed to work on, such as my footwork, which may not have been as sharp last year as it could have been. But I'm convinced that at this stage of my career, cricket is a mind game; you don't suddenly lose technique. I've got to get my head clear. What I want to do is enjoy my cricket, which is something that I've always tried to do. Maybe last season I didn't do enough of that.

In early August I was invited out to the Olympic Stadium in Sydney to help promote the fact that in February 2003 an ING Cup match will be played at the venue. I was quietly reminded that if I'm not a part of the

There's no doubt in my mind that one day we'll see a full house at Sydney's Olympic Stadium for a cricket match. This shot was played before a much smaller audience, during a media event staged to announce that during the 2002–03 Australian season an ING Cup one-dayer will be played where Cathy Freeman won Olympic gold.

World Cup squad I'll probably be playing in the match, and quickly the reporters started asking the same how-do-you-feel-about-not-being-in-the-one-day-side questions again. Then I was asked what I thought of cricket moving away, if only temporarily, from its usual Sydney home, the Sydney Cricket Ground. I think the scribes, who see me as an arch traditionalist, expected me to be a bit reticent, but I see no reason not to use alternative venues, as long as they are good enough for players and supporters. And there is no doubt that the Olympic Stadium is a state-of-the-art venue. The fact that the stands can be moved to create a genuine cricket oval, allied to the fact that in recent times it has been demonstrated that you can transplant high-quality turf pitches into just about any situation, adds up, in my eyes, to an opportunity too good for NSW Cricket to ignore.

This question about the quality of the wicket at this 'non-cricket' location reminded me that my preparation for the upcoming Tests against Pakistan was in trouble. By this time, early August, it was clear that the tour would not be going ahead, at least not to Pakistan, which was — in most people's eyes — just too dangerous, too politically unstable for a mere cricket tour. Still strong in my mind were the images of a bus having been blown up outside the New Zealand team's hotel in Karachi in May, and of Black Caps captain Stephen Fleming's emotional reaction when he tried to describe what it was like immediately after, when he didn't know where all his teammates were. In such situations you really have to be guided by governments and foreign affairs departments, who have a much better idea than we cricketers as to which parts of the cricket world are not safe to visit. And their advice was that we should stay away.

The mail was that the Tests would be played somewhere, but no one knew for sure where 'somewhere' was, with locations as diverse as England, Sharjah, Morocco, Kenya, Sri Lanka, Bangladesh and northern Australia all suggested. Eventually the Pakistan Cricket Board proposed and the Australian Cricket Board agreed that the first Test would be played at Colombo in Sri Lanka, and Tests two and three of the series at Sharjah in the United Arab Emirates. This will be the first time since 1912 that Australia has played a Test on a neutral venue. There would be no lead-up games, which made it particularly hard for those members of the Australian squad such as me who are not in the one-day teams, and who had not played any quality cricket over the winter.

**Kent Spitfires v Leicestershire Foxes, Norwich Union League
Division One, St Lawrence Ground Canterbury, 21 August**

Leicestershire 7–168 (45 overs: ND Burns 35; MJ Saggers 3–22) lost to Kent 5–172
(44.4 overs: SR Waugh 59 not out, PA Nixon 33 not out) by five wickets

**Kent v Leicestershire, Frizzell County Championship
Division One, St Lawrence Ground Canterbury, 22–25 August**

Leicestershire 259 (91 overs: IJ Sutcliffe 125; MJ Saggers 4–68) and 530
(138.5 overs: TR Ward 66, DL Maddy 156, PAJ DeFreitas 94; MM Patel 4–99)
drew with Kent 379 (109.2 overs: ET Smith 87, PA Nixon 86, MM Patel 82,
SR Waugh 16; J Srinath 4–70) and 0–58 (16 overs). Kent 11 points,
Leicestershire 9 points

A COUPLE OF WEEKS FURTHER into August and I was on the other side of the
world, here in Canterbury, being introduced to the British media as a short-
term signing for Kent. Everything had happened in a rush; once I realised
that I'd be short of practice before the Pakistan Tests I started to look for

I think this photograph was taken just after I'd been asked if I was in England to spy on the Poms
before the 2002–03 Ashes series.

alternatives — and then we heard that a few counties might be looking for replacements for overseas professionals who would be required by their nations for one-day matches in late August and September. Mark Waugh had already agreed to go back to Essex, where he'd played in the late '80s and early '90s, and there seemed to be opportunities at Kent (who were losing Andrew Symonds to the Australia A side), Northamptonshire (Mike Hussey) and Gloucestershire (Ian Harvey).

But if I was feeling bemused as I answered questions at a well-attended and well-organised media conference conducted at the St Lawrence Ground in Canterbury it was not because of the speed this new relationship had come about. Rather, I was being grilled about comments made by the former England coach now commentator David Lloyd, who had reputedly tagged my signing with Kent as being an example of 'glasnost gone mad'. The insinuation was that it was wrong for the English game to help out an Australian, especially with an Ashes series only months away. Lloyd then went on, so the story went, to complain

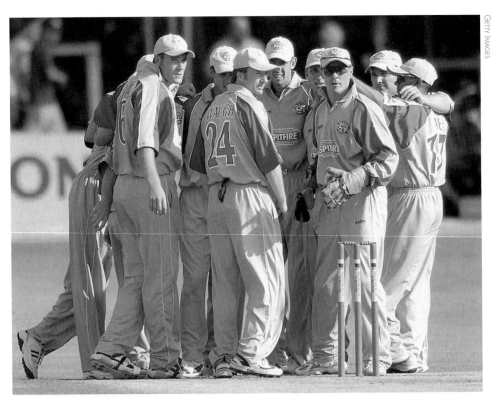

I had to get accustomed to the Kent boys forming a team huddle after each wicket, and linking arm-in-arm in celebration and thought. It was something that caught me by surprise initially, but when in Rome you do as the Romans do.

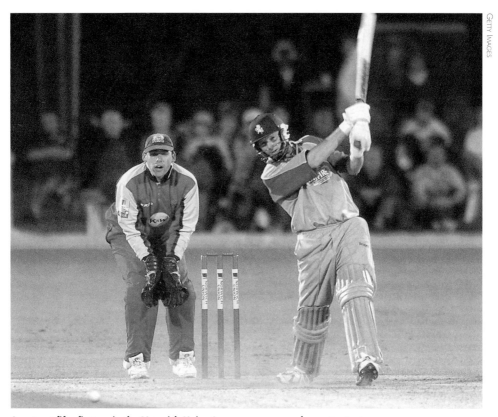

A not-out fifty first up in the Norwich Union League was a good way to start.

that while Australian cricketers could arrive in England at the drop of a hat there was next to no chance of an Australian state offering a similar benefit to an English player.

A day later, and the press was now reporting that Lloyd reckoned that my presence would benefit county cricket. 'He's a world-class player who will enrich county cricket,' he said, 'just as overseas signings like Barry Richards, Gordon Greenidge and Clive Lloyd did more than 30 years ago.' He actually called me to say that he had been taken out of context, which I happily accepted. However, for me, the confusion reflected once again the lack of accountability of some sections of the media. There was no apology from whoever instigated the non-story; instead it bubbled along for a few days even though it wasn't based on fact.

The main criticism of my time here revolves around the allegation that I'm on some sort of spying mission; that I'll be casting an eye over the main candidates for the Ashes tour and devising plans to bring their campaign unstuck. But that is an absurd argument: with so much cricket on television these days I could have quite easily stayed in the comfort of my home —

and close to my family — and at the same time made a detailed assessment of the England XI. I could even listen to the many pieces of inside information given out by the commentators. Without leaving Australian shores, I am able to collect data and vision on the strengths and weaknesses of each player, via live action and countless replays.

I'm here in England because I received an offer to come and play for Kent at a time when I definitely needed some quality hit-outs as a lead-up to the Pakistan series. The opportunity to help the county, and to make sure the side plays well, will add to the experience. My last game of cricket before I arrived here was the third Test against South Africa in Durban five months ago. Without these matches in England, I would have had no games — repeat, no games — leading into the Pakistan Tests, and I don't really fancy facing Waqar Younis and Shoaib Akhtar without some solid practice behind me.

Inevitably, I've been asked many questions about the upcoming Australia v England encounter, and I always respond immediately with the thought that is uppermost in my mind — that I can't wait for the opportunity to play the old enemy again. This will be my ninth Ashes battle, and for me the magic remains as it was back in my first series, in 1986–87. We lost that one, but have prevailed every time since — on this occasion I have a suspicion that the contest will be an excellent one, with the England squad containing a few impressive performers who we haven't seen in previous Ashes contests.

When I first ran into Devon Malcolm, back in the late '80s, he was a raw but very quick Derbyshire paceman. These days he's a Leicestershire bowler and still very dangerous, as I found out painfully during my maiden first-class innings for Kent.

The batting star of the 2002 English summer has been Michael Vaughan of Yorkshire, who missed the 2001 Ashes series through injury but has been a prolific run-scorer in recent Tests against Sri Lanka and India. Vaughan and Marcus Trescothick form a quality opening pair, capable of giving

I watch on as Phil DeFreitas, another former England Test bowler now playing for Leicestershire, fields off his own bowling.

England a solid platform to make competitive totals. Both men are energetic, ambitious and skilful, and have new-found belief in themselves at the top level, which is crucial to success.

Another relative newcomer to the England squad who has impressed me is the paceman Matthew Hoggard, a real trier, a '100 per cent man' who keeps on running in ball after ball and, as such, has to be respected. As well as Hoggard, who now seems established in the Test XI, the Poms have unearthed two exciting pace-bowling prospects in Simon Jones and Stephen Harmison, who both have the potential to do well on the faster, bouncier pitches in Australia.

For now, however, I was not so concerned with these players, but with the bowling attack of Leicestershire, our opponents in a Norwich Union League day-nighter at the St Lawrence Ground. And I couldn't have hoped for a better start. A big, boisterous crowd turned up — estimated at around 7500 (it could have been more judging by the long traffic jams on the roads into the ground) — on a brilliant night. And despite dropping to 4–52 and 5–97 chasing 168 — on an awkward pitch with temporary lights that made batting extremely difficult — we got home with two balls to spare. And I was there at the end, hitting the winning runs, a four forward of point, and finishing 59 not out. I'd batted for 86 balls, having taken a leaf out of Michael Bevan's book. Bevo is a disciple of the principle that if you're there at the end of an awkward runchase, when the odds were initially against you, then you've given yourself the best chance to win the game. This result left us third on the ladder, behind Worcestershire and Glamorgan, and still with a rough outside chance of taking the title.

Hitting the winning runs was a perfect beginning as it gave me an immediate connection with the supporters, who after the match called me out onto the balcony for an 'encore'. Believe me, this was a long way from what I had envisaged when I walked out to bat, having had only one hit on turf since Durban. It was tough going at the start, before my timing and foot movement came back to me. There were also nerves to deal with — no matter how many games you've played, they are always present. For me, they were heightened with the expectations that accompany being the overseas professional. And batting with partners you've only just met is a challenging task — you need to establish how quick your new comrades are between wickets, whether or not they like a chat at the end of the over, how much interaction they need between deliveries. Fortunately, we managed okay.

Of course, it was always going to be difficult to follow up this fairytale beginning, and soon it was time for the wicked witch to intervene and bring everyone back to reality. By the end of my first four-day game for Kent, which began the day after that thrilling one-dayer, we'd been left with some serious work to do if we were going to maintain our second place on the County Championship ladder.

This was a game in which we dropped 10 catches, fielded for nearly three-quarters of the match and suffered our fair share of injuries. It was also an encounter that offered me a real insight into what county cricket is all about, both good and bad.

The morning of the first day of the match was certainly much more relaxed than what we are accustomed to in Australia; perhaps the constant grind of unrelenting travel, practice and playing caused this less intense warm-up. Pre-match planning was minimal, mainly because it seemed everyone was familiar with everyone else's games, and I was struck by the lack of nerves and energy among the players. It seemed this

Another example of cricket's fluctuating fortunes. One night I'm hitting an unbeaten half-century amid wild applause to get us home in a thrilling one-dayer; soon after I'm walking off the field in silence — retired hurt during my first-class debut for Kent.

was just another game, though it must be said that my experience here was just one snapshot in time and might not accurately reflect the energies and activities that exist at other points of the season.

Once we'd begun, with Leicestershire batting first after winning the toss on an excellent wicket, one aspect of play that did take me a little by surprise was the interaction and chat between the players. If Australia had been involved it would have been termed 'sledging'. To me, it was just good-humoured banter and it kept rolling along, providing incentive to both sides as we battled to gain the ascendancy. It must also be said that quite a fair percentage of this talk was aimed at teammates rather than opponents. The Kent opening bowler, Amjad Khan, who is Danish, born in Copenhagen, has the most nicknames I've ever come across. As he walked back to his mark you could hear calls such as 'C'mon Kelphead' or 'C'mon Seaweed head' or 'Upside down head', 'Tutankhamen', 'King Tut' and 'Mr Tickle', to name just a few. I'm sure this type of humour plays a huge part in building up the team's unity and camaraderie during a long season. If you can't have a laugh at yourself and your fellow players then that fun element, so crucial to success, is gone.

The standard of play on the field was close to that you see nowadays in the Pura Cup in Australia. There were six internationals on show, which guaranteed intense competitiveness and quality. For the most part the cricketers were proactive, the cricket positive, until — on the final day — the crucial point of the game arrived. Unfortunately, this was the moment when I was reminded that old habits can die hard. Or maybe the fact that Leicestershire decided to bat out the last day was not so much a reflection on the philosophy of their captain, Iain Sutcliffe (who'd made a solid hundred in their first innings) but rather an indictment of the points system, which is lopsided to the point that it encourages draws ahead of victories.

The system is this: 12 points for a win, plus any points you earn in the first innings. Six points each for a tie, four each for a draw, plus any points earned in the first innings. In the first innings, you can claim up to four batting points (one for a total between 200 and 249, two if you total between 250 and 299, three if you total between 300 and 349, four if you total more than 350) and three bowling points (three or four wickets taken gains you one point, five to seven wickets gets you two points, eight to 10 gets you three points). Those four points for a draw seem to me to be way too many, especially in a competition in which three teams get relegated to division two at the end of the season. The system breeds caution at a time in the game's history when it is being clearly demonstrated by the world's top teams that bold aggressive cricket is the best way to get the results you're after.

Leicestershire worked their way to an overall lead of 275 runs, with 45 overs still available. It was perfectly set up for an exciting finale. Unfortunately, it wasn't to be. The loss of those four points for a draw was too much of a disincentive, so the match petered out to a dull draw with part-time bowlers operating at the end, to make sure no penalties were conceded because of slow over rates. There was some big hitting — the former international all-rounder Phil DeFreitas smashed 94 from 86 balls — but no thrills. It was such a shame — both sides had the potential to make this a quality finish. And I must stress that my criticism is not just about entertaining the crowd (though that should be a consideration). You can learn so much by being aggressive in such situations, by backing yourself and your teammates. Most times, there is much more to be gained, long term, by having a real go and losing than by playing safe and winning nothing.

Unfortunately, printing deadlines mean that this is where I have to draw the line on this book. Tomorrow, while the Australian one-day team is in Nairobi preparing for a game the following day against Kenya (and still savouring, no doubt, a big first-up thrashing of Pakistan), I'll be at Worcester playing in a Norwich Union League match. Three days later, I return to Taunton — where I played county cricket back in 1987 and 1988 — for an important County Championship match and then another one-dayer. There are games against Lancashire, Glamorgan and Yorkshire, and then I'm off to Sri Lanka for the first Test against Pakistan, then to Sharjah and then home for another Ashes series. Will I be in South Africa after that? Only time can tell.

I bear some scars from what has happened to me over the past eight months, but the one that is most apparent right at this moment is a small cut across the index finger of my right hand. It came about during my one innings in the county game against Leicestershire, when my quest for a big knock came to a shuddering halt after an old foe by the name of Devon Malcolm crashed a delivery into my index finger. For a batsman at this level, facing a bowler of Malcolm's pace and skill, this is an everyday occurrence, but instantly I knew things weren't right. I removed my glove and came across a finger covered in blood, with a split right across it. It seemed stitches would be needed, so off I went — 'retired hurt' on my first-class debut for Kent, a far cry from the adulation of the balcony encore after the triumph in the one-dayer. I came back in at the fall of the next wicket, but only briefly, as Javagal Srinath, the Indian Test fast bowler, knocked me over for just 16.

This little demonstration of cricket's ups and down — hero for a night, retired hurt, out — spread over just a couple of days, reminded me yet again of what sport at the highest level is all about, of what really matters when it comes to measuring character and ability.

It's not so much how you perform and react when you're succeeding that counts. It's how you fight back from adversity.

STATISTICS

SCORES AND AVERAGES

ABOVE: The great spirit in the Australian squad goes far beyond the players you see on the field, so it was fantastic to share our success with our support crew and families in the dressing-room after the third Test against South Africa, in Sydney.

BELOW: Two weeks earlier, Brett Lee (LEFT) and Jason Gillespie were quick to get in the spirit of things at the team's annual Christmas party in Melbourne. Little did they know about the roller-coaster ride that was in store for the Australian team over the following few weeks.

THE SOUTH AFRICANS IN AUSTRALIA, 2001–02
AUSTRALIA v SOUTH AFRICA, FIRST TEST
Adelaide Oval — 14–18 December 2001 (five-day match)
Toss: Australia • Umpires: SJA Taufel and S Venkataraghavan (Ind)
TV Umpire: SJ Davis • Match Referee: RS Madugalle (SL)

Australia first innings

JL Langer c Pollock b Henderson	116
ML Hayden c Ntini b Klusener	31
RT Ponting run out (Dippenaar/Boucher)	54
ME Waugh c Boucher b Hayward	2
*SR Waugh c McKenzie b Henderson	8
DR Martyn not out	124
+AC Gilchrist c Hayward b Henderson	7
SK Warne b Klusener	41
B Lee c McKenzie b Hayward	32
JN Gillespie c Boucher b Henderson	3
GD McGrath b Hayward	5
Extras (lb 6, nb 10)	16
Total (all out, 141 overs, 574 mins)	439

Fall: 1–80 (Hayden, 21.2 ov), 2–182 (Ponting, 50.6 ov), 3–199 (ME Waugh, 55.3 ov), 4–211 (SR Waugh, 65.3 ov), 5–238 (Langer, 79.2 ov), 6–248 (Gilchrist, 81.5 ov), 7–332 (Warne, 105.2 ov), 8–409 (Lee, 132.4 ov), 9–434 (Gillespie, 139.2 ov), 10–439 (McGrath, 140.6 ov).
Bowling: Pollock 28–8–64–0 (6nb), Hayward 31–5–108–3 (4nb), Ntini 19–7–64–0, Kallis 16–1–37–0, Klusener 14–4–44–2, Henderson 33–4–116–4

Australia second innings

JL Langer c Boucher b Pollock	1
ML Hayden b Kallis	131
RT Ponting lbw b Kallis	25
ME Waugh c Boucher b Henderson	74
+AC Gilchrist c McKenzie b Kallis	22
*SR Waugh c Pollock b Henderson	13
DR Martyn not out	6
SK Warne b Henderson	6
Extras (b 8, lb 16, nb 7)	31
Total (7 wickets dec, 78.1 overs, 324 mins)	309

Fall: 1–8 (Langer, 4.1 ov), 2–66 (Ponting, 19.3 ov), 3–247 (Hayden, 63.3 ov), 4–273 (ME Waugh, 68.4 ov), 5–291 (Gilchrist, 71.4 ov), 6–303 (SR Waugh, 76.4 ov), 7–309 (Warne, 78.1 ov).
Bowling: Pollock 12–4–38–1 (3nb), Hayward 10–0–32–0 (3nb), Henderson 29.1–1–130–3, Kallis 15–2–45–3, Ntini 8–3–13–0, Klusener 4–0–27–0 (1nb)

South Africa first innings

HH Gibbs st Gilchrist b Warne	78
G Kirsten lbw b McGrath	47
HH Dippenaar c Ponting b McGrath	4
CW Henderson run out (McGrath/Lee)	30
JH Kallis lbw b McGrath	5
ND McKenzie lbw b Martyn	87
L Klusener b Warne	22
+MV Boucher c Langer b Warne	64
*SM Pollock c Gilchrist b Warne	0
M Ntini c Ponting b Warne	9
M Hayward not out	0
Extras (b 8, lb 9, nb 11)	28
Total (all out, 121.4 overs, 512 mins)	374

Fall: 1–87 (Kirsten, 30.4 ov), 2–93 (Dippenaar, 32.4 ov), 3–155 (Henderson, 52.2 ov), 4–178 (Gibbs, 61.4 ov), 5–178 (Kallis, 62.3 ov), 6–214 (Klusener, 69.2 ov), 7–355 (McKenzie, 114.6 ov), 8–356 (Pollock, 117.1 ov), 9–365 (Boucher, 119.5 ov), 10–374 (Ntini, 121.4 ov)
Bowling: McGrath 33–10–94–3 (3nb), Gillespie 23–7–57–0, Warne 39.4–9–113–5 (1nb), Lee 19–2–81–0 (6nb), ME Waugh 3–0–9–0, Martyn 4–2–3–1

South Africa second innings (target: 375 runs)

HH Gibbs c Langer b McGrath	9
G Kirsten c Ponting b Warne	7
HH Dippenaar c Warne b McGrath	0
JH Kallis not out	65
ND McKenzie lbw b McGrath	0
L Klusener c Warne b Gillespie	18
+MV Boucher c Gilchrist b Gillespie	0
*SM Pollock c Ponting b Warne	1
CW Henderson c Ponting b Warne	3
M Ntini b Lee	4
M Hayward c Gilchrist b Lee	12
Extras (b 4, lb 1, w 1, nb 3)	9
Total (all out, 67 overs, 280 mins)	128

Fall: 1–12 (Gibbs, 6.5 ov), 2–17 (Kirsten, 11.6 ov), 3–21 (Dippenaar, 16.1 ov), 4–21 (McKenzie, 16.3 ov), 5–54 (Klusener, 30.5 ov), 6–58 (Boucher, 32.3 ov), 7–67 (Pollock, 35.5 ov), 8–74 (Henderson, 41.6 ov), 9–113 (Ntini, 58.6 ov), 10–128 (Hayward, 66.6 ov)
Bowling: McGrath 14–8–13–3 (1nb), Gillespie 11–4–23–2 (1w), Warne 29–7–57–3 (2nb), Lee 12–3–29–2, Martyn 1–0–1–0

Result: Australia won by 246 runs
Man of the Match: SK Warne

Note
In these scorecards * indicates captain, + indicates wicketkeeper

AUSTRALIA v SOUTH AFRICA, SECOND TEST
Melbourne Cricket Ground — 26–29 December 2001 (five–day match)
Toss: Australia • **Umpires:** DB Hair and EA Nicholls (WI) • **TV Umpire:** RL Parry
Match Referee: RS Madugalle (SL)

South Africa first innings

HH Gibbs c Ponting b McGrath	14
G Kirsten b McGrath	10
HH Dippenaar c Hayden b Lee	26
JH Kallis c Gilchrist b Bichel	38
ND McKenzie lbw b Lee	67
L Klusener c & b Bichel	0
+MV Boucher c Bichel b ME Waugh	43
*SM Pollock not out	42
CW Henderson run out (Bichel)	5
AA Donald c Ponting b Lee	0
M Hayward c ME Waugh b Bichel	14
Extras (b 1, lb 10, nb 7)	18
Total (all out, 103.5 overs, 427 mins)	**277**

Fall: 1–24 (Gibbs, 14.2 ov), 2–36 (Kirsten, 18.2 ov), 3–59 (Dippenaar, 30.4 ov), 4–131 (Kallis, 59.3 ov), 5–131 (Klusener, 59.4 ov), 6–198 (Boucher, 77.5 ov), 7–220 (McKenzie, 89.1 ov), 8–225 (Henderson, 89.6 ov), 9–233 (Donald, 91.6 ov), 10–277 (Hayward, 103.5 ov)
Bowling: McGrath 26–8–70–2 (1nb), Lee 31–10–77–3, Bichel 19.5–6–44–3 (1nb), Warne 19–3–56–0 (5nb), ME Waugh 8–1–19–1

South Africa second innings

HH Gibbs c Gilchrist b Lee	21
G Kirsten c Ponting b Lee	10
HH Dippenaar c Hayden b Warne	23
JH Kallis run out (Martyn/Gilchrist)	99
ND McKenzie c Gilchrist b Warne	12
L Klusener lbw b McGrath	7
+MV Boucher c ME Waugh b Warne	0
*SM Pollock run out (Martyn)	18
CW Henderson c ME Waugh b McGrath	16
AA Donald b Bichel	7
M Hayward not out	0
Extras (b 4, nb 2)	6
Total (all out, 75.1 overs, 331 mins)	**219**

Fall: 1–24 (Kirsten, 5.2 ov), 2–37 (Gibbs, 9.5 ov), 3–74 (Dippenaar, 25.1 ov), 4–107 (McKenzie, 38.1 ov), 5–120 (Klusener, 45.5 ov), 6–121 (Boucher, 46.4 ov), 7–157 (Pollock, 55.5 ov), 8–192 (Henderson, 68.3 ov), 9–215 (Donald, 73.6 ov), 10–219 (Kallis, 75.1 ov)
Bowling: McGrath 21–6–43–2 (1nb), Lee 18–5–52–2, Warne 24–3–68–3, Bichel 12.1–0–52–1 (1nb)

Australia first innings

JL Langer c Klusener b Donald	85
ML Hayden c Donald b Henderson	138
RT Ponting c Kallis b Hayward	22
ME Waugh b Donald	34
*SR Waugh run out (Gibbs)	90
DR Martyn c Kallis b Pollock	52
+AC Gilchrist not out	30
SK Warne c Kirsten b Donald	1
B Lee c McKenzie b Hayward	3
AJ Bichel c Boucher b Pollock	5
GD McGrath lbw b Pollock	0
Extras (lb 17, w 1, nb 9)	27
Total (all out, 139 overs, 563 mins)	**487**

Fall: 1–202 (Langer, 55.5 ov), 2–267 (Ponting, 69.4 ov), 3–267 (Hayden, 70.2 ov), 4–348 (ME Waugh, 91.4 ov), 5–429 (SR Waugh, 115.6 ov), 6–462 (Martyn, 126.5 ov), 7–463 (Warne, 127.1 ov), 8–470 (Lee, 133.3 ov), 9–475 (Bichel, 134.5 ov), 10–487 (McGrath, 138.6 ov)
Bowling: Donald 29–5–103–3, Pollock 31–3–84–3 (6nb), Hayward 26–1–109–2 (2nb), Kallis 17–3–55–0 (1w), Henderson 29–3–108–1 (1nb), Klusener 7–1–11–0

Australia second innings (target: 10 runs)

JL Langer c Henderson b Pollock	7
ML Hayden not out	3
RT Ponting not out	0
Extras	0
Total (1 wicket, 3 overs, 14 mins)	**10**

Fall: 1–7 (Langer, 1.4 ov)
Bowling: Donald 2–0–4–0, Pollock 1–0–6–1

Result: Australia won by nine wickets
Man of the Match: ML Hayden

AUSTRALIA v SOUTH AFRICA, THIRD TEST
Sydney Cricket Ground — 2–5 January 2002 (five–day match)
Toss: Australia • Umpires: DJ Harper and DR Shepherd (Eng) • TV Umpire: SJA Taufel
Match Referee: RS Madugalle (SL)

Australia first innings
JL Langer c McKenzie b Boje	126
ML Hayden c Kallis b Pollock	105
RT Ponting run out (Ontong/Boucher)	14
ME Waugh c Boucher b Donald	19
*SR Waugh b Pollock	30
DR Martyn c McKenzie b Boje	117
+AC Gilchrist c Boucher b Kallis	34
SK Warne b Pollock	37
B Lee b Boje	29
SCG MacGill c Henderson b Boje	20
GD McGrath not out	1
Extras (b 4, lb 8, w 1, nb 9)	22
Total (all out, 144.2 overs, 554 mins)	554

Fall: 1–219 (Hayden, 61.3 ov), 2–247 (Ponting, 68.6 ov), 3–253 (Langer, 70.3 ov), 4–302 (SR Waugh, 84.3 ov), 5–308 (ME Waugh, 89.3 ov), 6–356 (Gilchrist, 105.4 ov), 7–439 (Warne, 118.6 ov), 8–502 (Lee, 136.5 ov), 9–542 (MacGill, 142.5 ov), 10–554 (Martyn, 144.2 ov)
Bowling: Donald 31–6–119–1 (1w), Pollock 37–11–109–3 (6nb), Kallis 22–1–129–1 (2nb), Henderson 27–3–112–0 (1nb), Boje 25.2–6–63–4, Ontong 2–0–10–0

Australia second innings (target: 53 runs)
JL Langer not out	30
ML Hayden not out	21
Extras (lb 2, nb 1)	3
Total (0 wickets, 10.1 overs, 44 mins)	54

Bowling: Donald 3–0–12–0, Pollock 3–1–11–0 (1nb), Boje 2.1–0–15–0, Henderson 2–0–14–0

South Africa first innings
HH Gibbs c ME Waugh b MacGill	32
G Kirsten c Ponting b McGrath	18
HH Dippenaar b McGrath	3
JH Kallis c Gilchrist b MacGill	4
ND McKenzie b Warne	20
JL Ontong lbw b Warne	9
+MV Boucher c Ponting b Warne	35
*SM Pollock c Martyn b McGrath	6
N Boje run out (Langer/McGrath)	7
CW Henderson c McGrath b MacGill	9
AA Donald not out	2
Extras (lb 8, nb 1)	9
Total (all out, 62.2 overs, 241 mins)	154

Fall: 1–37 (Kirsten, 13.1 ov), 2–43 (Dippenaar, 17.2 ov), 3–56 (Kallis, 20.4 ov), 4–77 (Gibbs, 26.3 ov), 5–93 (McKenzie, 37.3 ov), 6–98 (Ontong, 39.3 ov), 7–111 (Pollock, 44.3 ov), 8–121 (Boje, 46.5 ov), 9–148 (Boucher, 59.1 ov), 10–154 (Henderson, 62.2 ov)
Bowling: McGrath 17–6–35–3, Lee 6–2–13–0, MacGill 20.2–6–51–3 (1nb), Warne 19–5–47–3

South Africa second innings (following on)
HH Gibbs b Lee	10
G Kirsten b MacGill	153
HH Dippenaar c Ponting b MacGill	74
JH Kallis c Gilchrist b Warne	34
ND McKenzie c MacGill b Lee	38
JL Ontong lbw b Warne	32
+MV Boucher c Gilchrist b McGrath	27
*SM Pollock not out	61
N Boje b MacGill	1
CW Henderson b MacGill	2
AA Donald c Lee b Warne	2
Extras (b 8, lb 7, nb 3)	18
Total (all out, 141.5 overs, 525 mins)	452

Fall: 1–17 (Gibbs, 7.5 ov), 2–166 (Dippenaar, 49.3 ov), 3–211 (Kallis, 71.1 ov), 4–282 (McKenzie, 93.4 ov), 5–356 (Ontong, 113.4 ov), 6–372 (Kirsten, 118.4 ov), 7–392 (Boucher, 125.5 ov), 8–393 (Boje, 128.4 ov), 9–403 (Henderson, 132.2 ov), 10–452 (Donald, 141.5 ov)
Bowling: McGrath 28–5–95–1, Warne 42.5–8–132–3 (2nb), Lee 19–5–62–2 (1nb), MacGill 45–13–123–4, ME Waugh 6–1–14–0, Ponting 1–0–11–0

Result: Australia won by 10 wickets
Series: Australia won the series 3–0
Men of the Match: ML Hayden and JL Langer
Man of the Series: ML Hayden

THE VB SERIES, 2001–02

AUSTRALIA v NEW ZEALAND, GAME ONE

Melbourne Cricket Ground — 11 January 2002 (50-over match)
Toss: Australia • **Umpires:** DB Hair and RL Parry • **TV Umpire:** RG Patterson
Match Referee: Hanumant Singh (Ind)

New Zealand innings

L Vincent c SR Waugh b Lee	17
MH Richardson c Gilchrist b McGrath	8
*SP Fleming c ME Waugh b McGrath	1
CD McMillan c Gilchrist b Lee	17
CL Cairns c Ponting b Lee	10
SB Styris c & b Harvey	23
CZ Harris not out	63
+AC Parore run out (Martyn/Lee)	3
DL Vettori run out (Warne/Gilchrist)	30
JEC Franklin not out	9
Extras (lb 6, w 6, nb 6)	18
Total (8 wickets, 50 overs, 215 mins)	199

DNB: SE Bond

Fall: 1–20 (Richardson, 4.6 ov), 2–22 (Fleming, 8.6 ov), 3–41 (Vincent, 12.1 ov), 4–54 (Cairns, 14.5 ov), 5–67 (McMillan, 18.2 ov), 6–89 (Styris, 25.1 ov), 7–94 (Parore, 26.3 ov), 8–166 (Vettori, 42.6 ov)
Bowling: McGrath 10–1–47–2 (4nb, 1w), Williams 10–2–31–0, Lee 10–1–43–3 (2nb, 2w), Harvey 10–1–35–1, Warne 10–0–37–0 (3w)

Australia innings

+AC Gilchrist c & b Cairns	23
ME Waugh c Parore b Bond	1
RT Ponting c Franklin b Bond	45
MG Bevan c Franklin b Bond	27
*SR Waugh run out (Vincent/Parore)	15
DR Martyn lbw b Vettori	24
IJ Harvey b Cairns	5
SK Warne b Harris	3
B Lee b Cairns	0
BA Williams not out	13
GD McGrath c Parore b Vettori	7
Extras (b 1, w 3, nb 9)	13
Total (all out, 42 overs, 189 mins)	176

Fall: 1–5 (ME Waugh, 0.5 ov), 2–63 (Gilchrist, 8.1 ov), 3–98 (Ponting, 18.1 ov), 4–104 (Bevan, 20.1 ov), 5–135 (SR Waugh, 28.1 ov), 6–142 (Harvey, 30.3 ov), 7–150 (Warne, 33.4 ov), 8–151 (Lee, 34.4 ov), 9–168 (Martyn, 39.4 ov), 10–176 (McGrath, 41.6 ov)
Bowling: Bond 10–1–53–3 (3nb, 1w), Franklin 5–0–27–0 (3nb), Cairns 10–1–42–3 (2nb, 2w), Vettori 10–1–36–2, Harris 7–0–17–1 (1nb)

Result: New Zealand won by 23 runs
Man of the Match: CZ Harris

AUSTRALIA v SOUTH AFRICA, GAME TWO

Melbourne Cricket Ground — 13 January 2002 (50-over match)
Toss: Australia • **Umpires:** SJ Davis and SJA Taufel • **TV Umpire:** RL Parry
Match Referee: Hanumant Singh (Ind)

Australia innings

+AC Gilchrist c Donald b Pollock	0
ML Hayden c Klusener b Pollock	10
RT Ponting run out (Rhodes)	51
MG Bevan run out (Ntini)	10
*SR Waugh b Kallis	62
DR Martyn c McKenzie b Kallis	31
A Symonds c Gibbs b Kallis	0
SK Warne c Pollock b Klusener	4
B Lee c Rhodes b Donald	0
AJ Bichel lbw b Pollock	17
JN Gillespie not out	1
Extras (lb 6, w 6)	12
Total (all out, 48.5 overs, 212 mins)	198

Fall: 1–0 (Gilchrist, 0.1 ov), 2–39 (Hayden, 7.4 ov), 3–64 (Bevan, 15.4 ov), 4–106 (Ponting, 28.1 ov), 5–164 (Waugh, 40.1 ov), 6–164 (Symonds, 40.3 ov), 7–170 (Warne, 42.3 ov), 8–171 (Lee, 43.2 ov), 9–196 (Bichel, 47.6 ov), 10–198 (Martyn, 48.5 ov)
Bowling: Pollock 9–1–25–3, Donald 10–0–54–1 (4w), Kallis 9.5–1–30–3 (1w), Ntini 10–0–31–0 (1w), Klusener 7–0–33–1, Boje 3–0–19–0

South Africa innings

HH Gibbs c Gilchrist b Gillespie	38
G Kirsten c Gilchrist b Bichel	22
JH Kallis c Gilchrist b Gillespie	6
ND McKenzie c Symonds b Warne	34
JN Rhodes not out	43
L Klusener c Gilchrist b Lee	18
+MV Boucher c Symonds b Lee	11
*SM Pollock not out	5
Extras (b 2, lb 12, w 4, nb 4)	22
Total (6 wickets, 48.3 overs, 221 mins)	199

DNB: N Boje, AA Donald, M Ntini

Fall: 1–51 (Kirsten, 9.2 ov), 2–66 (Kallis, 14.5 ov), 3–71 (Gibbs, 16.6 ov), 4–136 (McKenzie, 36.2 ov), 5–169 (Klusener, 42.3 ov), 6–187 (Boucher, 46.1 ov)
Bowling: Lee 9.3–1–42–2 (2nb, 2w), Gillespie 10–3–28–2, Bichel 10–1–45–1 (1nb), Warne 10–1–19–1, Symonds 7–0–41–0 (1w), Bevan 2–0–10–0 (1nb, 1w)

Result: South Africa won by four wickets
Man of the Match: SM Pollock

NEW ZEALAND v SOUTH AFRICA, GAME THREE

Bellerive Oval, Hobart — 15 January 2002 (50-over match)
Toss: South Africa • Umpires: SJ Davis and DJ Harper • TV Umpire: JH Smeaton
Match Referee: Hanumant Singh (Ind)

South Africa innings

HH Gibbs c Fleming b Vettori	36
G Kirsten run out (Harris)	97
HH Dippenaar c McMillan b Bond	37
JN Rhodes c Harris b Cairns	13
ND McKenzie c Fleming b Franklin	22
L Klusener b Vettori	5
+MV Boucher not out	30
*SM Pollock run out (Styris)	0
JM Kemp not out	10
Extras (lb 3, w 1, nb 3)	7
Total (7 wickets, 50 overs, 204 mins)	257

DNB: AA Donald, M Ntini

Fall: 1–82 (Gibbs, 15.4 ov), 2–157 (Dippenaar, 32.4 ov), 3–178 (Rhodes, 36.2 ov), 4–194 (Kirsten, 40.4 ov), 5–215 (McKenzie, 44.3 ov), 6–217 (Klusener, 45.1 ov), 7–217 (Pollock, 45.2 ov)
Bowling: Bond 10–0–64–1, Franklin 8–0–42–1 (2nb, 1w), Cairns 10–0–54–1, Vettori 10–0–37–2 (1nb), Harris 10–0–43–0, Styris 2–0–14–0

Result: South Africa won by 26 runs
Man of the Match: G Kirsten

New Zealand innings

L Vincent c Pollock b Ntini	23
MH Richardson c Klusener b Donald	8
*SP Fleming c Dippenaar b Klusener	85
CD McMillan c Gibbs b Kemp	36
CL Cairns b Ntini	11
SB Styris c Boucher b Klusener	9
CZ Harris c Dippenaar b Kemp	2
+AC Parore not out	21
DL Vettori c Kirsten b Donald	0
JEC Franklin c Boucher b Donald	2
SE Bond not out	17
Extras (b 3, lb 8, w 5, nb 1)	17
Total (9 wickets, 50 overs, 222 mins)	231

Fall: 1–10 (Richardson, 3.2 ov), 2–71 (Vincent, 16.2 ov), 3–152 (McMillan, 32.6 ov), 4–170 (Fleming, 37.3 ov), 5–181 (Cairns, 38.6 ov), 6–183 (Styris, 39.2 ov), 7–192 (Harris, 42.2 ov), 8–196 (Vettori, 43.2 ov), 9–202 (Franklin, 45.5 ov)
Bowling: Pollock 10–1–38–0, Donald 10–1–40–3, Ntini 10–0–36–2 (1nb, 1w), Kemp 10–0–50–2 (3w), Klusener 10–0–56–2 (1w)

AUSTRALIA v NEW ZEALAND, GAME FOUR

Sydney Cricket Ground — 17 January 2002 (50-over match)
Toss: New Zealand • Umpires: RL Parry and SJA Taufel • TV Umpire: DB Hair
Match Referee: Hanumant Singh (Ind)

New Zealand innings

MH Richardson st Campbell b Warne	26
BB McCullum run out (Lee)	5
L Vincent c Ponting b Harvey	24
CD McMillan c Campbell b Martyn	39
*CL Cairns c SR Waugh b Gillespie	31
SB Styris c Bevan b Harvey	20
CZ Harris not out	42
+AC Parore c ME Waugh b Warne	18
DL Vettori c Campbell b Lee	2
JEC Franklin run out (Lee)	5
Extras (b 2, lb 18, w 3)	23
Total (9 wickets, 50 overs, 213 mins)	235

DNB: SE Bond

Fall: 1–13 (McCullum, 5.3 ov), 2–54 (Vincent, 20.6 ov), 3–74 (Richardson, 23.6 ov), 4–135 (McMillan, 33.4 ov), 5–137 (Cairns, 34.3 ov), 6–182 (Styris, 42.1 ov), 7–210 (Parore, 45.6 ov), 8–216 (Vettori, 47.5 ov), 9–235 (Franklin, 49.6 ov)
Bowling: McGrath 10–2–22–0, Gillespie 10–0–28–1 (1w), Harvey 10–0–40–2 (1w), Lee 8–1–40–1, Warne 9–0–65–2 (1w), Martyn 3–0–20–1

Australia innings

ME Waugh run out (Vincent)	0
+RJ Campbell c Harris b Vettori	38
RT Ponting c Parore b Bond	11
MG Bevan c Styris b Cairns	66
*SR Waugh c Harris b Bond	9
DR Martyn run out (Cairns)	24
IJ Harvey c Vincent b Harris	6
SK Warne c Richardson b Harris	14
B Lee lbw b Franklin	1
JN Gillespie not out	13
GD McGrath c Vincent b Harris	1
Extras (lb 7, w 18, nb 4)	29
Total (all out, 47.2 overs, 208 mins)	212

Fall: 1–1 (ME Waugh, 1.2 ov), 2–29 (Ponting, 6.3 ov), 3–98 (Campbell, 21.2 ov), 4–118 (SR Waugh, 25.2 ov), 5–174 (Bevan, 38.1 ov), 6–178 (Martyn, 40.1 ov), 7–181 (Harvey, 41.2 ov), 8–188 (Lee, 42.3 ov), 9–203 (Warne, 45.5 ov), 10–212 (McGrath, 47.2 ov)
Bowling: Bond 8–1–28–2 (1nb, 7w), Franklin 9–0–46–1 (2nb, 5w), Cairns 9–2–32–1 (2w), Vettori 10–0–45–1, Harris 8.2–0–37–3 (1nb, 2w), Styris 3–0–17–0 (2w)

Result: New Zealand won by 23 runs
Man of the Match: CZ Harris

NEW ZEALAND v SOUTH AFRICA, GAME FIVE

The Gabba, Brisbane — 19 January 2002 (50-over match)
Toss: South Africa • Umpires: SJ Davis and DB Hair • TV Umpire: PD Parker
Match Referee: Hanumant Singh (Ind)

South Africa innings	
HH Gibbs b Franklin	0
G Kirsten c & b Harris	43
JH Kallis c Vincent b Bond	65
JN Rhodes c Harris b Cairns	44
HH Dippenaar run out (Bond)	7
+MV Boucher c Franklin b Bond	51
*SM Pollock c Parore b Franklin	15
JM Kemp c Parore b Cairns	1
JL Ontong c McMillan b Bond	4
S Elworthy c Cairns b Bond	0
M Ntini not out	2
Extras (lb 6, w 2, nb 1)	9
Total (all out, 48.3 overs, 192 mins)	241

Fall: 1–0 (Gibbs, 0.1 ov), 2–115 (Kirsten, 21.4 ov), 3–115 (Kallis, 22.1 ov), 4–131 (Dippenaar, 25.5 ov), 5–204 (Rhodes, 39.6 ov), 6–231 (Pollock, 44.3 ov), 7–234 (Kemp, 45.3 ov), 8–236 (Boucher, 46.2 ov), 9–237 (Elworthy, 46.5 ov), 10–241 (Ontong, 48.3 ov)
Bowling: Franklin 8–0–41–2 (1nb, 2w), Bond 9.3–0–37–4, Cairns 10–0–44–2, Vettori 10–0–58–0, Harris 10–0–45–1, McMillan 1–0–10–0

New Zealand innings	
MH Richardson c Ontong b Pollock	0
BB McCullum c Kallis b Ntini	37
L Vincent c Boucher b Pollock	9
*SP Fleming c Ontong b Kallis	23
CD McMillan b Pollock b Kallis	6
CL Cairns not out	102
CZ Harris lbw b Elworthy	24
+AC Parore not out	21
Extras (lb 8, w 8, nb 6)	22
Total (6 wickets, 49.1 overs, 203 mins)	244
DNB: DL Vettori, JEC Franklin, SE Bond	

Fall: 1–0 (Richardson, 0.2 ov), 2–31 (Vincent, 10.3 ov), 3–71 (Fleming, 17.5 ov), 4–73 (McCullum, 18.5 ov), 5–98 (McMillan, 23.3 ov), 6–160 (Harris, 37.1 ov)
Bowling: Pollock 9.1–2–29–2, Elworthy 10–0–47–1 (4w), Ntini 8–0–46–1 (2nb), Kallis 10–0–57–2 (2w), Ontong 5–0–26–0 (1w), Kemp 7–0–31–0 (1w)

Result: New Zealand won by four wickets
Man of the Match: CL Cairns

AUSTRALIA v SOUTH AFRICA, GAME SIX

The Gabba, Brisbane — 20 January 2002 (50-over match)
Toss: Australia • Umpires: DJ Harper and SJA Taufel • TV Umpire: PD Parker
Match Referee: Hanumant Singh (Ind)

Australia innings	
ME Waugh c Boucher b Elworthy	15
ML Hayden c Kirsten b Elworthy	10
RT Ponting c Gibbs b Klusener	80
DR Martyn not out	104
A Symonds c Rhodes b Boje	3
*SR Waugh not out	22
Extras (w 2, nb 5)	7
Total (4 wickets, 50 overs, 196 mins)	241
DNB: +AC Gilchrist, SK Warne, AJ Bichel, JN Gillespie, GD McGrath	

Fall: 1–25 (ME Waugh, 9.4 ov), 2–29 (Hayden, 11.5 ov), 3–200 (Ponting, 42.2 ov), 4–205 (Symonds, 43.6 ov)
Bowling: Pollock 10–1–28–0, Elworthy 10–1–53–2 (1w), Langeveldt 5–0–31–0 (1nb), Kallis 7–0–38–0 (2nb), Klusener 8–0–48–1 (2nb), Boje 10–0–43–1 (1w)

Result: Australia won by 27 runs
Man of the Match: DR Martyn

South Africa innings	
HH Gibbs c Bichel b McGrath	18
G Kirsten c Gilchrist b McGrath	22
JH Kallis lbw b Gillespie	37
ND McKenzie c Gilchrist b Gillespie	68
JN Rhodes c Gilchrist b Symonds	2
+MV Boucher c & b Symonds	10
*SM Pollock c Hayden b Symonds	18
L Klusener b Bichel	16
N Boje b McGrath	1
S Elworthy not out	11
CK Langeveldt b McGrath	3
Extras (lb 1, w 6, nb 1)	8
Total (all out, 48.4 overs, 202 mins)	214

Fall: 1–34 (Gibbs, 6.6 ov), 2–49 (Kirsten, 12.3 ov), 3–126 (Kallis, 28.1 ov), 4–135 (Rhodes, 31.2 ov), 5–153 (Boucher, 35.5 ov), 6–175 (McKenzie, 40.4 ov), 7–191 (Pollock, 43.4 ov), 8–199 (Klusener, 45.4 ov), 9–204 (Boje, 46.6 ov), 10–214 (Langeveldt, 48.4 ov)
Bowling: McGrath 9.4–0–30–4 (1nb), Gillespie 10–1–60–2 (5w), Bichel 9–1–27–1 (1w), Warne 10–1–48–0, Symonds 10–0–48–3

AUSTRALIA v SOUTH AFRICA, GAME SEVEN

Sydney Cricket Ground — 22 January 2002 (50-over match)
Toss: South Africa • Umpires: DB Hair and DJ Harper • TV Umpire: SJA Taufel
Match Referee: Hanumant Singh (Ind)

South Africa innings

HH Gibbs c Gilchrist b McGrath	0
G Kirsten lbw b Warne	44
HH Dippenaar c Warne b McGrath	0
ND McKenzie b Bichel	18
JN Rhodes c Gilchrist b Bichel	0
+MV Boucher lbw b Bichel	1
*SM Pollock lbw b Bichel	0
L Klusener lbw b Gillespie	0
N Boje not out	13
S Elworthy c SR Waugh b McGrath	18
M Ntini c & b Bichel	0
Extras (lb 3, w 9)	12
Total (all out, 38.3 overs, 161 mins)	106

Australia innings

ME Waugh not out	55
+AC Gilchrist b Pollock	8
RT Ponting b Klusener	33
DR Martyn not out	6
Extras (lb 1, w 1, nb 3)	5
Total (2 wickets, 18.4 overs, 78 mins)	107

DNB: *SR Waugh, MG Bevan, A Symonds, SK Warne, AJ Bichel, JN Gillespie, GD McGrath

Fall: 1–1 (Gibbs, 0.2 ov), 2–5 (Dippenaar, 2.2 ov), 3–42 (McKenzie, 16.5 ov), 4–44 (Rhodes, 18.2 ov), 5–49 (Boucher, 20.4 ov), 6–49 (Pollock, 20.6 ov), 7–50 (Klusener, 21.3 ov), 8–79 (Kirsten, 29.3 ov), 9–103 (Elworthy, 36.6 ov), 10–106 (Ntini, 38.3 ov)
Bowling: McGrath 10-1-29-3 (3w), Gillespie 9-1-27-1 (1w), Symonds 4-0-7-0 (1w), Bichel 6.3-0-19-5 (1w), Warne 6-1-13-1 (3w), ME Waugh 3-0-8-0

Fall: 1–24 (Gilchrist, 4.6 ov), 2–101 (Ponting, 18.1 ov)
Bowling: Pollock 7-0-36-1 (1nb, 1w), Ntini 7-2-36-0 (1nb), Klusener 2.4-0-28-1 (1nb), Boje 2-0-6-0

Result: Australia won by eight wickets
Man of the Match: AJ Bichel

NEW ZEALAND v SOUTH AFRICA, GAME EIGHT

Adelaide Oval — 27 January 2002 (50-over match)
Toss: South Africa • Umpires: DJ Harper and RL Parry • TV Umpire: SJ Davis
Match Referee: Hanumant Singh (Ind)

South Africa innings

HH Gibbs b Cairns	89
G Kirsten c Parore b Bond	0
JH Kallis c Parore b Cairns	30
ND McKenzie c Parore b Vettori	5
JN Rhodes c Fleming b Franklin	55
+MV Boucher not out	57
*SM Pollock not out	4
Extras (b 2, lb 6, w 5)	13
Total (5 wickets, 50 overs, 188 mins)	253

DNB: JL Ontong, N Boje, M Ntini, AA Donald

New Zealand innings

BB McCullum lbw b Kallis	29
NJ Astle c Boucher b Pollock	0
L Vincent c Donald b Pollock	20
*SP Fleming c Gibbs b Donald	43
CD McMillan c Ontong b Boje	16
CL Cairns c Rhodes b Boje	9
CZ Harris not out	9
+AC Parore b Boje	7
DL Vettori c Ontong b Boje	0
JEC Franklin lbw b Donald	2
SE Bond c Donald b Ntini	9
Extras (b 3, lb 7, w 4, nb 2)	16
Total (all out, 45.2 overs, 192 mins)	160

Fall: 1–9 (Kirsten, 3.2 ov), 2–74 (Kallis, 21.5 ov), 3–93 (McKenzie, 26.3 ov), 4–156 (Gibbs, 41.2 ov), 5–242 (Rhodes, 48.5 ov)
Bowling: Franklin 10-0-39-1 (1w), Bond 10-0-47-1 (3w), Cairns 10-0-69-2, Vettori 10-0-34-1, Harris 10-0-56-0 (1w)

Result: South Africa won by 93 runs
Man of the Match: MV Boucher

Fall: 1–1 (Astle, 0.4 ov), 2–37 (Vincent, 10.6 ov), 3–59 (McCullum, 17.4 ov), 4–102 (McMillan, 29.1 ov), 5–130 (Cairns, 35.6 ov), 6–134 (Fleming, 38.3 ov), 7–145 (Parore, 41.1 ov), 8–145 (Vettori, 41.3 ov), 9–148 (Franklin, 42.2 ov), 10–160 (Bond, 45.2 ov)
Bowling: Pollock 8-0-24-2, Ntini 9.2-1-32-1 (1nb, 1w), Kallis 6-0-18-1 (2w), Donald 10-0-37-2 (1w), Boje 10-0-31-4, Ontong 2-0-8-0 (1nb)

AUSTRALIA v NEW ZEALAND, GAME NINE

Adelaide Oval — 26 January 2002 (50-over match)
Toss: New Zealand • Umpires: SJ Davis and SJA Taufel • TV Umpire: DJ Harper
Match Referee: Hanumant Singh (Ind)

New Zealand innings

BB McCullum c Gilchrist b McGrath	0
NJ Astle b McGrath	95
L Vincent c Symonds b ME Waugh	55
CD McMillan c & b ME Waugh	8
*SP Fleming st Gilchrist b Warne	13
CL Cairns not out	39
CZ Harris not out	19
Extras (lb 8, w 5)	13
Total (5 wickets, 50 overs, 203 mins)	242

DNB: +AC Parore, DJ Nash, DL Vettori, SE Bond

Fall: 1–0 (McCullum, 0.3 ov), 2–128 (Vincent, 27.5 ov), 3–152 (McMillan, 33.4 ov), 4–176 (Fleming, 39.5 ov), 5–197 (Astle, 44.3 ov)
Bowling: McGrath 10–3–36–2, Gillespie 10–1–40–0 (2w), Warne 10–1–33–1, Bichel 6–0–57–0, Symonds 6–0–30–0 (1w), ME Waugh 8–0–38–2 (2w)

Australia innings

+AC Gilchrist b Bond	21
ME Waugh c & b Nash	0
RT Ponting c Parore b Bond	0
DR Martyn c Vincent b Bond	2
*SR Waugh c Fleming b Vettori	30
MG Bevan c Bond b Harris	45
A Symonds c McCullum b Harris	11
SK Warne c Parore b Cairns	22
AJ Bichel c Astle b Bond	7
JN Gillespie b Bond	15
GD McGrath not out	6
Extras (lb 1, w 2, nb 3)	6
Total (all out, 45.2 overs, 189 mins)	165

Fall: 1–7 (ME Waugh, 0.6 ov), 2–8 (Ponting, 1.3 ov), 3–25 (Martyn, 5.5 ov), 4–26 (Gilchrist, 7.2 ov), 5–97 (SR Waugh, 24.6 ov), 6–106 (Bevan, 27.2 ov), 7–114 (Symonds, 29.4 ov), 8–139 (Bichel, 37.3 ov), 9–154 (Warne, 41.4 ov), 10–165 (Gillespie, 45.2 ov)
Bowling: Nash 8–1–31–1 (1nb, 1w), Bond 9.2–2–25–5 (1nb, 1w), Cairns 6–0–19–1, Vettori 10–0–44–1, Astle 2–0–10–0, Harris 10–0–35–2 (1nb)

Result: New Zealand won by 77 runs
Man of the Match: SE Bond

AUSTRALIA v NEW ZEALAND, GAME 10

Melbourne Cricket Ground — 29 January 2002 (50-overs match)
Toss: New Zealand • Umpires: DB Hair and SJA Taufel • TV Umpire: RG Patterson
Match Referee: Hanumant Singh (Ind)

New Zealand innings

L Vincent c Gilchrist b McGrath	5
NJ Astle c Warne b Lee	11
*SP Fleming run out (SR Waugh/Warne)	50
CD McMillan c Ponting b Harvey	34
CL Cairns c Bevan b Warne	55
CZ Harris run out (Warne/Harvey)	41
DJ Nash run out (Harvey)	24
+AC Parore lbw McGrath	1
AR Adams not out	13
DL Vettori not out	0
Extras (lb 4, w 4, nb 3)	11
Total (8 wickets, 50 overs, 206 minutes)	245

DNB: SE Bond

Fall: 1–7 (Vincent, 2.6 ov), 2–19 (Astle, 5.5 ov), 3–73 (McMillan, 16.4 ov), 4–143 (Fleming, 32.3 ov), 5–178 (Cairns, 40.2 ov), 6–226 (Nash, 47.4 ov), 7–228 (Parore, 48.2 ov), 8–235 (Harris, 49.4 ov)
Bowling: McGrath 10–0–41–2, Lee 8–0–32–1 (2w), Bichel 6–0–20–0, Warne 10–0–56–1 (1nb, 2w), Harvey 10–0–59–1, SR Waugh 6–0–33–0 (2nb)

Australia innings

ME Waugh c Adams b Nash	21
+AC Gilchrist b Bond	14
RT Ponting c Astle b Bond	8
DR Martyn c Harris b Adams	6
*SR Waugh c Parore b Nash	7
MG Bevan not out	102
IJ Harvey c Parore b Bond	12
SK Warne c Bond b Adams	29
B Lee c Astle b Bond	27
AJ Bichel not out	13
Extras (w 3, nb 6)	9
Total (8 wickets, 49.3 overs, 233 mins)	248

DNB: GD McGrath

Fall: 1–24 (Gilchrist, 3.3 ov), 2–40 (Ponting, 7.2 ov), 3–51 (ME Waugh, 13.6 ov), 4–53 (Martyn, 14.3 ov), 5–65 (SR Waugh, 17.1 ov), 6–82 (Harvey, 21.3 ov), 7–143 (Warne, 36.4 ov), 8–224 (Lee, 47.3 ov)
Bowling: Nash 9–0–50–2 (3nb), Bond 9.3–2–38–4 (1nb, 1w), Adams 10–0–52–2 (2nb), Vettori 10–0–36–0 (1w), Harris 8–0–50–0 (1w), Astle 3–0–22–0

Result: Australia won by two wickets
Man of the Match: MG Bevan

NEW ZEALAND v SOUTH AFRICA, GAME 11
WACA Ground, Perth — 1 February 2002 (50-over match)
Toss: New Zealand • Umpires: DB Hair and DJ Harper • TV Umpire: RL Parry
Match Referee: Hanumant Singh (Ind)

South Africa innings

HH Gibbs c Fleming b Nash	8
G Kirsten c Vincent b Franklin	0
JH Kallis b Nash	11
ND McKenzie b Nash	3
JN Rhodes not out	107
+MV Boucher c Astle b Harris	58
*SM Pollock not out	69
Extras (lb 5, w 4, nb 5)	14
Total (5 wickets, 50 overs, 208 mins)	270

DNB: N Boje, JM Kemp, AA Donald, M Ntini

Fall: 1–10 (Kirsten, 2.6 ov), 2–14 (Gibbs, 5.6 ov),
3–23 (McKenzie, 7.6 ov), 4–35 (Kallis, 11.6 ov),
5–173 (Boucher, 40.5 ov)
Bowling: Franklin 10-0-65-1 (3nb, 2w), Nash
10-0-37-3 (1nb, 1w), Adams 10-0-57-0 (1nb),
Styris 8-0-43-0, Vettori 4-0-21-0, McMillan 3-0-15-0,
Harris 5-0-27-1

New Zealand innings

L Vincent c Boucher b Donald	22
NJ Astle c Kallis b Ntini	0
AR Adams c Boucher b Ntini	10
*SP Fleming c Boucher b Kallis	27
CD McMillan c Kirsten b Pollock	46
SB Styris c Kemp b Pollock	12
CZ Harris lbw b Boje	0
DJ Nash c Gibbs b Donald	12
+AC Parore not out	36
DL Vettori not out	20
Extras (lb 9, w 5, nb 4)	18
Total (8 wickets, 50 overs, 216 mins)	203

DNB: JEC Franklin

Fall: 1–4 (Astle, 1.3 ov), 2–22 (Adams, 5.4 ov),
3–61 (Vincent, 13.4 ov), 4–72 (Fleming, 16.6 ov),
5–129 (McMillan, 25.2 ov), 6–130 (Styris, 27.6 ov),
7–130 (Harris, 28.2 ov), 8–156 (Nash, 37.5 ov)
Bowling: Pollock 10-1-55-2 (3nb), Ntini 10-1-23-2,
Kallis 10-1-44-1 (3w), Donald 10-2-35-2,
Kemp 2-0-18-0 (2w), Boje 8-0-19-1

Result: South Africa won by 67 runs
Man of the Match: JN Rhodes

AUSTRALIA v SOUTH AFRICA, GAME 12
WACA Ground, Perth — 3 February 2002 (50-over match)
Toss: South Africa • Umpires: SJ Davis and RL Parry • TV Umpire: DB Hair
Match Referee: Hanumant Singh (Ind)

Australia innings

+AC Gilchrist b Ntini	31
ME Waugh c Kallis b Donald	34
RT Ponting run out (Gibbs)	26
DR Martyn c Boucher b Boje	29
*SR Waugh b Boje	42
MG Bevan c Pollock b Ntini	1
DS Lehmann not out	49
SK Warne b Pollock	0
B Lee not out	51
Extras (b 1, lb 12, w 6, nb 1)	20
Total (7 wickets, 50 overs, 218 mins)	283

DNB: AJ Bichel, GD McGrath

Fall: 1–47 (Gilchrist, 9.3 ov), 2–76 (ME Waugh, 13.4 ov),
3–117 (Ponting, 22.1 ov), 4–150 (Martyn, 30.4 ov),
5–157 (Bevan, 31.5 ov), 6–194 (SR Waugh, 38.5 ov),
7–195 (Warne, 39.4 ov)
Bowling: Pollock 9-0-44-1, Ntini 10-1-58-2 (1nb),
Kallis 9-0-52-0, Donald 9-2-62-1 (1w),
Boje 10-0-38-2 (5w), Klusener 3-0-16-0

South Africa innings

HH Gibbs c Bevan b Bichel	34
G Kirsten c Martyn b Lee	10
JH Kallis not out	104
HH Dippenaar c Gilchrist b McGrath	33
JN Rhodes c Martyn b Lehmann	20
+MV Boucher c Bichel b Lehmann	12
L Klusener not out	25
Extras (lb 1, w 6, nb 5)	12
Total (5 wickets, 50 overs, 221 mins)	250

DNB: N Boje, *SM Pollock, AA Donald, M Ntini

Fall: 1–30 (Kirsten, 9.4 ov), 2–66 (Gibbs, 18.3 ov),
3–129 (Dippenaar, 30.6 ov), 4–172 (Rhodes, 39.4 ov),
5–198 (Boucher, 43.1 ov)
Bowling: McGrath 10-3-21-1, Lee 10-1-66-1
(1nb, 3w), Bichel 9-0-38-1 (2nb), Warne 10-0-53-0,
Bevan 2-0-17-0 (2nb, 1w), SR Waugh 4-0-26-0 (1w),
Lehmann 5-0-28-2 (1w)

Result: Australia won by 33 runs
Man of the Match: JH Kallis

NEW ZEALAND v SOUTH AFRICA, FIRST FINAL

Melbourne Cricket Ground — 6 February 2002 (50-over match)
Toss: New Zealand • **Umpires:** DJ Harper and SJA Taufel • **TV Umpire:** RL Parry
Match Referee: Hanumant Singh (Ind)

New Zealand innings

L Vincent c Rhodes b Ntini	7
NJ Astle c Kallis b Ntini	9
*SP Fleming c Kallis b Klusener	50
CD McMillan run out (Gibbs)	73
CL Cairns c Kirsten b Klusener	0
CZ Harris c Boucher b Pollock	9
DJ Nash c Donald b Ntini	9
+AC Parore c Boucher b Ntini	2
AR Adams c Klusener b Ntini	13
DL Vettori not out	6
SE Bond run out (Rhodes)	1
Extras (lb 5, w 6)	11
Total (all out, 47.5 overs, 206 mins)	190

South Africa innings

HH Gibbs c Parore b Cairns	24
G Kirsten run out (McMillan)	25
JH Kallis not out	59
HH Dippenaar not out	79
Extras (lb 1, w 1, nb 2)	4
Total (2 wickets, 45.1 overs, 172 mins)	191

DNB: JN Rhodes, +MV Boucher, L Klusener, N Boje, *SM Pollock, AA Donald, M Ntini

Fall: 1–15 (Vincent, 5.2 ov), 2–18 (Astle, 7.1 ov), 3–127 (Fleming, 32.1 ov), 4–128 (Cairns, 32.6 ov), 5–155 (Harris, 38.4 ov), 6–158 (McMillan, 40.1 ov), 7–168 (Nash, 43.1 ov), 8–168 (Parore, 43.2 ov), 9–187 (Adams, 45.5 ov), 10–190 (Bond, 47.5 ov)
Bowling: Pollock 9–0–30–1, Ntini 10–0–31–5 (3w), Donald 8–0–44–0 (1w), Kallis 6.5–0–25–0 (2w), Klusener 7–0–27–2, Boje 7–0–28–0

Fall: 1–51 (Kirsten, 13.1 ov), 2–52 (Gibbs, 14.5 ov)
Bowling: Bond 8–2–21–0, Nash 1–0–6–0, Adams 8–0–32–0 (1w), Vettori 5–0–32–0, Cairns 8–1–27–1 (2nb), McMillan 3–0–14–0, Harris 9.1–0–44–0, Astle 3–0–14–0

Result: South Africa won by eight wickets
Man of the Match: M Ntini

NEW ZEALAND v SOUTH AFRICA, SECOND FINAL

Sydney Cricket Ground — 8 February 2002 (50-over match)
Toss: New Zealand • **Umpires:** SJ Davis and SJA Taufel • **TV Umpire:** DJ Harper
Match Referee: Hanumant Singh (Ind)

New Zealand innings (46 overs maximum)

L Vincent c Ntini b Kallis	43
NJ Astle c Klusener b Pollock	7
AR Adams c Boucher b Ntini	1
*SP Fleming c Dippenaar b Donald	17
CD McMillan c Ntini b Kallis	0
CL Cairns c Boje b Kallis	57
CZ Harris lbw b Klusener	31
+AC Parore c Gibbs b Klusener	0
DL Vettori lbw b Donald	3
JEC Franklin lbw b Donald	0
SE Bond not out	5
Extras (b 2, lb 1, w 8)	11
Total (all out, 41.1 overs, 177 mins)	175

South Africa innings (target: 172 from 46 overs)

HH Gibbs b Adams	46
G Kirsten c Parore b Bond	2
JH Kallis c Parore b Adams	10
HH Dippenaar c Parore b Cairns	29
JN Rhodes not out	61
+MV Boucher not out	16
Extras (lb 1, w 6, nb 2)	9
Total (4 wickets, 38.1 overs, 149 mins)	173

DNB: L Klusener, *SM Pollock, N Boje, AA Donald, M Ntini

Fall: 1–15 (Astle, 6.1 ov), 2–17 (Adams, 7.3 ov), 3–68 (Vincent, 13.4 ov), 4–68 (Fleming, 14.2 ov), 5–72 (McMillan, 15.3 ov), 6–147 (Harris, 34.4 ov), 7–147 (Parore, 34.5 ov), 8–157 (Vettori, 38.1 ov), 9–157 (Franklin, 38.2 ov), 10–175 (Cairns, 41.1 ov)
Bowling: Pollock 6–2–24–1, Ntini 7–2–45–1 (1w), Donald 8–0–29–3 (3w), Kallis 5.1–0–23–3 (3w), Boje 8–0–21–0, Klusener 7–0–30–2 (1w)

Fall: 1–50 (Kirsten, 8.1 ov), 2–65 (Kallis, 13.2 ov), 3–68 (Gibbs, 15.3 ov), 4–141 (Dippenaar, 36.1 ov)
Bowling: Bond 8–2–31–1 (3w), Franklin 4–0–29–0 (1nb, 3w), Vettori 4.1–0–25–0, Adams 8–0–33–2, Cairns 7–1–32–1, Astle 2–0–5–0, Harris 5–0–17–0 (1nb)

Result: South Africa won by six wickets (D/L method)
Series: South Africa won the best-of-three finals 2–0
Man of the Match: JN Rhodes
Man of the Series: SE Bond

THE AUSTRALIANS IN SOUTH AFRICA, 2002

SOUTH AFRICA A v AUSTRALIANS

North West Cricket Stadium, Potchefstroom — 17–19 February 2002 (three-day match)
Toss: Australians • Umpires: IL Howell and RE Koertzen

Australians first innings

JL Langer b Hall	12
ML Hayden lbw b Hall	18
RT Ponting c Tsolekile b Bodi	120
ME Waugh c Prince b Henderson	62
*SR Waugh not out	102
DR Martyn c Cullinan b Henderson	1
+AC Gilchrist c Smith b Hall	16
SK Warne lbw b Hall	0
B Lee c Smith b Hall	6
JN Gillespie not out	5
Extras (lb 8, w 7, nb 9)	24
Total (8 wickets dec., 98.5 overs, 399 mins)	366

DNB: GD McGrath

Fall: 1–39 (Hayden, 17.2 ov), 2–52 (Langer, 19.1 ov), 3–177 (ME Waugh, 50.1 ov), 4–271 (Ponting, 69.1 ov), 5–272 (Martyn, 72.4 ov), 6–319 (Gilchrist, 85.6 ov), 7–321 (Warne, 87.4 ov), 8–332 (Lee, 89.4 ov)
Bowling: Nel 25–5–75–0 (1nb), Langeveldt 12–4–46–0 (1nb), Hall 25–7–97–5 (3nb, 5w), Henderson 19–3–74–2 (1nb), Benkenstein 4–1–15–0 (1nb), Bodi 13.5–1–51–1 (2nb, 2w)

Australians second innings

JL Langer c Prince b Henderson	45
ML Hayden c Smith b Henderson	39
DR Martyn not out	10
B Lee c Tsolekile b Henderson	0
+AC Gilchrist not out	0
Extras (w 1)	1
Total (3 wickets, 27 overs, 93 mins)	95

Fall: 1–77 (Hayden, 15.1 ov), 2–94 (Langer, 23.3 ov), 3–94 (Lee, 25.5 ov)
Bowling: Nel 3–0–14–0 (1w), Henderson 13–6–41–3, Benkenstein 5–0–26–0, Bodi 6–1–14–0

South Africa A first innings

GC Smith c Ponting b McGrath	0
JA Rudolph b McGrath	14
AG Prince c ME Waugh b McGrath	92
DJ Cullinan c Gilchrist b McGrath	4
*DM Benkenstein c Hayden b Warne	0
AJ Hall c ME Waugh b Warne	18
GH Bodi c Gillespie b Lee	33
+TL Tsolekile b Lee	0
CW Henderson c Langer b McGrath	7
CK Langeveldt c sub (DS Lehmann) b Gillespie	10
A Nel not out	2
Extras (b 4, nb 6)	10
Total (all out, 68 overs, 291 mins)	190

Fall: 1–0 (Smith, 0.6 ov), 2–35 (Rudolph, 13.2 ov), 3–40 (Cullinan, 15.5 ov), 4–66 (Benkenstein, 19.2 ov), 5–114 (Hall, 35.5 ov), 6–162 (Bodi, 44.4 ov), 7–162 (Tsolekile, 44.6 ov), 8–175 (Henderson, 53.5 ov), 9–184 (Prince, 61.3 ov), 10–190 (Langeveldt, 67.6 ov)
Bowling: McGrath 15–9–17–5 (1nb), Gillespie 17–6–44–1, Lee 15–2–55–2 (3nb), Warne 16–2–59–2 (2nb), ME Waugh 1–0–4–0, Martyn 4–2–7–0

Result: Match drawn

SOUTH AFRICA v AUSTRALIA, FIRST TEST

New Wanderers Stadium, Johannesburg — 22–24 February 2002 (five-day match)
Toss: Australia • Umpires: SA Bucknor (WI) and RE Koertzen • TV Umpire: IL Howell
Match Referee: CW Smith (WI)

Australia first innings

JL Langer lbw b Donald	28
ML Hayden c Boucher b Nel	122
RT Ponting c Boucher b Nel	39
ME Waugh c Boucher b Ntini	53
*SR Waugh c Gibbs b Kallis	32
DR Martyn c Kirsten b Kallis	133
+AC Gilchrist not out	204
SK Warne c McKenzie b Boje	12
B Lee not out	4
Extras (b 2, lb 14, w 4, nb 5)	25
Total (7 wickets dec., 146 overs, 626 mins)	652

DNB: JN Gillespie, GD McGrath

Fall: 1–46 (Langer, 10.4 ov), 2–113 (Ponting, 23.1 ov),
3–224 (ME Waugh, 50.4 ov), 4–272 (Hayden, 67.2 ov),
5–293 (SR Waugh, 79.1 ov), 6–610 (Martyn, 141.2 ov),
7–643 (Warne, 144.3 ov)
Bowling: Donald 15.2–2–72–1 (1w), Ntini 33–8–124–1
(2nb, 2w), Kallis 24–1–116–2 (1w), Nel 30.4–6–121–2
(3nb), Boje 35–4–153–1, McKenzie 8–0–50–0

South Africa first innings

HH Gibbs lbw b Warne	34
G Kirsten c Warne b McGrath	1
AG Prince c Hayden b Gillespie	49
JH Kallis c Warne b Lee	3
ND McKenzie c Gillespie b McGrath	16
HH Dippenaar c Gilchrist b McGrath	2
*+MV Boucher c Gilchrist b Lee	23
N Boje c ME Waugh b Gillespie	0
M Ntini c SR Waugh b Lee	9
A Nel lbw b Warne	7
AA Donald not out	3
Extras (b 4, lb 3, nb 5)	12
Total (all out, 48 overs, 230 mins)	159

Fall: 1–11 (Kirsten, 2.1 ov), 2–51 (Gibbs, 15.3 ov),
3–55 (Kallis, 16.6 ov), 4–108 (McKenzie, 26.6 ov),
5–113 (Prince, 33.5 ov), 6–113 (Dippenaar, 34.6 ov),
7–114 (Boje, 37.5 ov), 8–146 (Ntini, 44.1 ov),
9–155 (Boucher, 46.1 ov), 10–159 (Nel, 47.6 ov)
Bowling: McGrath 14–6–28–3, Gillespie 15–5–58–2,
Warne 9–0–26–2, Lee 10–1–40–3 (5nb)

South Africa second innings (following on)

HH Gibbs st Gilchrist b Warne	47
G Kirsten c Martyn b Gillespie	12
AG Prince b Warne	28
JH Kallis c Gilchrist b McGrath	8
ND McKenzie not out	27
HH Dippenaar lbw b Warne	1
*+MV Boucher b Warne	1
N Boje c Ponting b McGrath	5
M Ntini b McGrath	0
A Nel c Langer b McGrath	0
AA Donald c Hayden b McGrath	0
Extras (w 1, nb 3)	4
Total (all out, 38.3 overs, 176 mins)	133

Fall: 1–20 (Kirsten, 7.1 ov), 2–89 (Prince, 23.3 ov),
3–98 (Gibbs, 27.2 ov), 4–98 (Kallis, 28.5 ov),
5–107 (Dippenaar, 31.1 ov), 6–109 (Boucher, 31.6 ov),
7–122 (Boje, 36.1 ov), 8–122 (Ntini, 36.2 ov),
9–122 (Nel, 36.4 ov), 10–133 (Donald, 38.3 ov)
Bowling: McGrath 12.3–4–21–5, Lee 10–2–55–0
(2nb, 1w), Gillespie 4–1–13–1, Warne 12–3–44–4 (1nb)

Result: Australia won by an innings and 360 runs
Man of the Match: AC Gilchrist

SOUTH AFRICA A v AUSTRALIANS
St George's Park, Port Elizabeth — 1–3 March 2002 (four-day match)
Toss: Australians • Umpires: RE Koertzen and MZ Nanabhay

South Africa A first innings

GC Smith c Lee b Watson	28
JA Rudolph c Gilchrist b MacGill	36
M van Jaarsveld c Gilchrist b Gillespie	11
*DJ Cullinan lbw b Watson	86
HM Amla b Lee	81
JM Kemp b Bichel	16
RJ Peterson c Gilchrist b Lee	6
GH Bodi lbw b Lee	2
+TL Tsolekile not out	0
D Pretorius b Lee	0
CM Willoughby c Gilchrist b Bichel	7
Extras (b 1, lb 10, w 3, nb 14)	28
Total (all out, 92.3 overs, 367 mins)	301

Fall: 1–58 (Smith, 16.3 ov), 2–86 (Rudolph, 26.5 ov), 3–96 (van Jaarsveld, 29.3 ov), 4–251 (Cullinan, 76.4 ov), 5–283 (Amla, 85.4 ov), 6–285 (Kemp, 86.2 ov), 7–288 (Bodi, 87.3 ov), 8–294 (Peterson, 89.1 ov), 9–294 (Pretorius, 89.2 ov), 10–301 (Willoughby, 92.3 ov)
Bowling: Gillespie 15–4–33–1, Lee 14–3–37–4 (2w), Watson 16–5–40–2 (3nb), Bichel 16.3–1–82–2 (11nb, 1w), MacGill 28–5–94–1, ME Waugh 3–1–4–0

South Africa A second innings

GC Smith b MacGill	31
JA Rudolph c Gilchrist b Lee	11
M van Jaarsveld b MacGill	29
*DJ Cullinan lbw b Bichel	19
HM Amla b Bichel	2
JM Kemp c Gilchrist b Lee	56
RJ Peterson c MacGill b Watson	9
GH Bodi c SR Waugh b MacGill	45
+TL Tsolekile lbw b Bichel	6
D Pretorius b MacGill	7
CM Willoughby not out	0
Extras (b 1, lb 1, nb 15)	17
Total (all out, 60.3 overs, 254 mins)	232

Fall: 1–31 (Rudolph, 9.1 ov), 2–70 (Smith, 22.3 ov), 3–82 (van Jaarsveld, 24.2 ov), 4–96 (Amla, 27.3 ov), 5–107 (Cullinan, 29.1 ov), 6–127 (Peterson, 34.5 ov), 7–214 (Bodi, 54.2 ov), 8–219 (Kemp, 55.3 ov), 9–228 (Tsolekile, 59.5 ov), 10–232 (Pretorius, 60.3 ov)
Bowling: Gillespie 8–4–23–0, Lee 13–1–32–2 (8nb), MacGill 22.3–4–114–4, Bichel 11–1–41–3 (3nb), Watson 6–0–20–1

Australians first innings

JL Langer c van Jaarsveld b Willoughby	161
DS Lehmann lbw b Pretorius	60
RT Ponting c Kemp b Willoughby	40
ME Waugh b Pretorius	110
*SR Waugh c Tsolekile b Pretorius	4
SR Watson not out	100
+AC Gilchrist c van Jaarsveld b Pretorius	56
B Lee c Cullinan b Pretorius	0
AJ Bichel c Amla b Willoughby	9
JN Gillespie run out (Smith/Kemp)	15
SCG MacGill not out	0
Extras (b 4, lb 2, w 1, nb 12)	19
Total (9 wickets dec, 116.2 overs, 477 mins)	574

Fall: 1–103 (Lehmann, 30.2 ov), 2–180 (Ponting, 42.4 ov), 3–387 (ME Waugh, 82.6 ov), 4–387 (Langer, 83.4 ov), 5–391 (SR Waugh, 86.6 ov), 6–490 (Gilchrist, 102.3 ov), 7–490 (Lee, 102.6 ov), 8–515 (Bichel, 107.3 ov), 9–563 (Gillespie, 115.2 ov)
Bowling: Pretorius 29–1–148–5 (3nb, 1w), Willoughby 29–4–101–3 (3nb), Kemp 24–5–106–0 (1nb), Bodi 14.2–0–85–0 (4nb), Peterson 20–0–128–0 (1nb)

Result: Australians won by an innings and 41 runs

SOUTH AFRICA v AUSTRALIA, SECOND TEST

Newlands, Cape Town — 8–12 March 2002 (five-day match)
Toss: South Africa • Umpires: SA Bucknor (WI) and RE Koertzen • TV Umpire: DL Orchard
Match Referee: CW Smith (WI)

South Africa first innings
HH Gibbs c ME Waugh b Gillespie	12
G Kirsten c ME Waugh b Lee	7
GC Smith c Ponting b McGrath	3
JH Kallis c Gilchrist b McGrath	23
ND McKenzie b Warne	20
AG Prince c Gilchrist b McGrath	10
*+MV Boucher c Gilchrist b Lee	26
AJ Hall c Gilchrist b Gillespie	70
PR Adams c Warne b Gillespie	35
M Ntini c ME Waugh b Warne	14
D Pretorius not out	5
Extras (b 4, lb 5, nb 5)	14
Total (all out, 80 overs, 355 mins)	239

Fall: 1–15 (Gibbs, 3.5 ov), 2–18 (Smith, 6.2 ov), 3–25 (Kirsten, 8.4 ov), 4–70 (McKenzie, 21.3 ov), 5–73 (Kallis, 26.3 ov), 6–92 (Prince, 34.1 ov), 7–147 (Boucher, 50.5 ov), 8–216 (Adams, 74.3 ov), 9–229 (Hall, 78.6 ov), 10–239 (Ntini, 79.6 ov)
Bowling: McGrath 20–4–42–3, Gillespie 15–4–52–3, Lee 16–1–65–2 (5nb), Warne 28–10–70–2, ME Waugh 1–0–1–0

South Africa second innings
HH Gibbs c Ponting b Warne	39
G Kirsten lbw b Lee	87
GC Smith c Gilchrist b Warne	68
JH Kallis lbw b Warne	73
ND McKenzie run out (Martyn)	99
AG Prince c Ponting b Warne	20
*+MV Boucher lbw b Gillespie	37
AJ Hall run out (Lee/Gillespie)	0
PR Adams not out	23
M Ntini c Langer b Warne	11
D Pretorius c ME Waugh b Warne	0
Extras (b 8, lb 3, w 2, nb 3)	16
Total (all out, 162 overs, 686 mins)	473

Fall: 1–84 (Gibbs, 29.1 ov), 2–183 (Kirsten, 60.6 ov), 3–254 (Smith, 79.3 ov), 4–284 (Kallis, 91.5 ov), 5–350 (Prince, 121.6 ov), 6–431 (Boucher, 142.4 ov), 7–433 (Hall, 146.1 ov), 8–440 (McKenzie, 150.4 ov), 9–464 (Ntini, 159.2 ov), 10–473 (Pretorius, 161.6 ov)
Bowling: McGrath 25–7–56–0 (1w), Gillespie 29–10–81–1 (1w), Warne 70–15–161–6 (3nb), Lee 22–3–99–1, ME Waugh 9–3–34–0, Martyn 4–0–15–0, SR Waugh 3–0–16–0

Australia first innings
JL Langer b Ntini	37
ML Hayden c Hall b Kallis	63
RT Ponting c Boucher b Adams	47
ME Waugh c Gibbs b Ntini	25
*SR Waugh b Adams	0
DR Martyn c Boucher b Ntini	2
+AC Gilchrist not out	138
SK Warne c Kallis b Adams	63
B Lee c Prince b Kallis	0
JN Gillespie c Kallis b Adams	0
GD McGrath lbw b Ntini	2
Extras (b 2, lb 1, w 2)	5
Total (all out, 80.5 overs, 353 mins)	382

Fall: 1–67 (Langer, 12.2 ov), 2–130 (Hayden, 26.5 ov), 3–162 (Ponting, 39.2 ov), 4–168 (SR Waugh, 41.4 ov), 5–176 (ME Waugh, 44.5 ov), 6–185 (Martyn, 46.6 ov), 7–317 (Warne, 69.5 ov), 8–338 (Lee, 72.2 ov), 9–343 (Gillespie, 75.2 ov), 10–382 (McGrath, 80.5 ov)
Bowling: Ntini 22.5–5–93–4, Pretorius 11–1–72–0, Kallis 16–1–65–2 (1w), Hall 11–1–47–0, Adams 20–1–102–4 (1w)

Australia second innings (target: 331 runs)
JL Langer b Pretorius	58
ML Hayden c Boucher b Kallis	96
RT Ponting not out	100
ME Waugh c Boucher b Ntini	16
*SR Waugh b Adams	14
DR Martyn lbw b Adams	0
+AC Gilchrist c McKenzie b Kallis	24
SK Warne not out	15
Extras (lb 6, nb 5)	11
Total (6 wickets, 79.1 overs, 366 mins)	334

Fall: 1–102 (Langer, 22.1 ov), 2–201 (Hayden, 47.4 ov), 3–251 (ME Waugh, 58.1 ov), 4–268 (SR Waugh, 65.3 ov), 5–268 (Martyn, 67.4 ov), 6–305 (Gilchrist, 74.1 ov)
Bowling: Ntini 24–4–90–1, Pretorius 14–5–60–1 (3nb), Adams 21.1–0–104–2, Hall 3–0–6–0 (1nb), Kallis 17–2–68–2 (1nb)

Result: Australia won by four wickets
Man of the Match: SK Warne

SOUTH AFRICA v AUSTRALIA, THIRD TEST

Kingsmead, Durban — 15–18 March 2002 (five-day match)
Toss: South Africa • **Umpires:** DL Orchard and S Venkataraghavan (Ind)
TV Umpire: IL Howell • **Match Referee:** CW Smith (WI)

Australia first innings

JL Langer c Kirsten b Terbrugge	11
ML Hayden c McKenzie b Kallis	28
RT Ponting run out (Gibbs)	89
ME Waugh c Smith b Kallis	45
*SR Waugh c Boucher b Adams	7
DR Martyn b Terbrugge	11
+AC Gilchrist c Smith b Adams	91
SK Warne c Boucher b Ntini	26
B Lee b Ntini	0
JN Gillespie c Boucher b Hall	1
GD McGrath not out	4
Extras (w 2)	2
Total (all out, 74.1 overs, 338 mins)	315

Fall: 1–11 (Langer, 1.1 ov), 2–61 (Hayden, 13.6 ov), 3–169 (Ponting, 35.4 ov), 4–178 (ME Waugh, 39.4 ov), 5–182 (SR Waugh, 42.1 ov), 6–230 (Martyn, 51.6 ov), 7–287 (Warne, 64.4 ov), 8–289 (Lee, 66.3 ov), 9–311 (Gilchrist, 73.1 ov), 10–315 (Gillespie, 74.1 ov)
Bowling: Ntini 20–3–87–2, Terbrugge 16–2–61–2, Kallis 20–3–95–2 (2w), Hall 9.1–2–35–1, Adams 9–0–37–2

Australia second innings

JL Langer c Boucher b Terbrugge	18
ML Hayden c Prince b Terbrugge	0
RT Ponting c Terbrugge b Ntini	34
ME Waugh b Kallis	30
*SR Waugh c Kallis b Ntini	42
DR Martyn c Boucher b Kallis	0
+AC Gilchrist c Boucher b Kallis	16
SK Warne c McKenzie b Adams	13
JN Gillespie c Kallis b Adams	3
B Lee not out	23
GD McGrath b Ntini	0
Extras (b 1, lb 3, w 1, nb 2)	7
Total (all out, 49 overs, 224 mins)	186

Fall: 1–4 (Hayden, 1.6 ov), 2–19 (Langer, 3.6 ov), 3–77 (Ponting, 14.1 ov), 4–90 (ME Waugh, 18.2 ov), 5–90 (Martyn, 18.6 ov), 6–114 (Gilchrist, 26.1 ov), 7–129 (Warne, 29.5 ov), 8–150 (Gillespie, 37.3 ov), 9–186 (SR Waugh, 48.5 ov), 10–186 (McGrath, 48.6 ov)
Bowling: Ntini 17–2–65–3 (2nb, 1w), Terbrugge 4–1–21–2, Hall 4–1–20–0, Adams 13–0–47–2, Kallis 11–2–29–3

South Africa first innings

HH Gibbs c Gilchrist b Gillespie	51
G Kirsten c Gilchrist b Lee	21
PR Adams c Hayden b Lee	6
GC Smith c Gilchrist b McGrath	1
JH Kallis c & b Warne	16
ND McKenzie c Martyn b Lee	25
AG Prince c Lee b Warne	0
*+MV Boucher c & b Warne	0
AJ Hall not out	27
M Ntini c McGrath b Warne	14
DJ Terbrugge c Gilchrist b Lee	0
Extras (lb 1, w 1, nb 4)	6
Total (all out, 55.2 overs, 258 mins)	167

Fall: 1–48 (Kirsten, 11.5 ov), 2–74 (Adams, 19.5 ov), 3–75 (Smith, 20.5 ov), 4–85 (Gibbs, 24.4 ov), 5–109 (Kallis, 31.5 ov), 6–119 (Prince, 39.2 ov), 7–119 (Boucher, 39.6 ov), 8–148 (McKenzie, 51.2 ov), 9–167 (Ntini, 54.2 ov), 10–167 (Terbrugge, 55.2 ov)
Bowling: McGrath 11–4–26–1, Lee 17.2–1–82–4 (4nb, 1w), Gillespie 14–6–25–1, Warne 13–4–33–4

South Africa second innings (target: 335 runs)

HH Gibbs c Martyn b ME Waugh	104
G Kirsten run out (Martyn/Lee)	64
GC Smith c Gilchrist b ME Waugh	42
JH Kallis not out	61
ND McKenzie c Hayden b Warne	4
AG Prince c ME Waugh b Warne	48
*+MV Boucher not out	8
Extras (lb 2, w 2, nb 5)	9
Total (5 wickets, 104.5 overs, 449 mins)	340

Fall: 1–142 (Kirsten, 43.3 ov), 2–216 (Smith, 66.3 ov), 3–218 (Gibbs, 68.3 ov), 4–232 (McKenzie, 73.1 ov), 5–331 (Prince, 103.3 ov)
Bowling: McGrath 28–11–54–0, Lee 20–2–75–0 (3nb, 2w), Gillespie 15–2–58–0, Warne 30–6–108–2 (2nb), ME Waugh 11.5–1–43–2

Result: South Africa won by five wickets
Series: Australia won the series 2–1
Man of the Match: HH Gibbs
Man of the Series: AC Gilchrist

THE SOUTH AFRICANS IN AUSTRALIA 2001–02, TEST AVERAGES

Australia Batting and Fielding

Name	Mat	Inn	NO	Runs	HS	Ave	SR	100	50	Ct	St
DR Martyn	3	4	2	299	124 *	149.50	59.56	2	1	1	–
ML Hayden	3	6	2	429	138	107.25	59.17	3	–	2	–
JL Langer	3	6	1	365	126	73.00	53.36	2	1	2	–
SR Waugh	3	4	0	141	90	35.25	51.45	–	1	–	–
ME Waugh	3	4	0	129	74	32.25	54.43	–	1	4	–
AC Gilchrist	3	4	1	93	34	31.00	63.69	–	–	9	1
RT Ponting	3	5	1	115	54	28.75	59.58	–	1	11	–
B Lee	3	3	0	64	32	21.33	39.26	–	–	1	–
SK Warne	3	4	0	85	41	21.25	63.90	–	–	2	–
SCG MacGill	1	1	0	20	20	20.00	86.95	–	–	1	–
AJ Bichel	1	1	0	5	5	5.00	83.33	–	–	2	–
GD McGrath	3	3	1	6	5	3.00	26.08	–	–	1	–
JN Gillespie	1	1	0	3	3	3.00	14.28	–	–	–	–

Australia Bowling

Name	Mat	O	M	R	W	Ave	Best	5wi	10wm	SR	ER
DR Martyn	3	5	2	4	1	4.00	1–3	–	–	30.0	0.80
AJ Bichel	1	32	6	96	4	24.00	3–44	–	–	48.0	3.00
SCG MacGill	1	65.2	19	174	7	24.85	4–123	–	–	56.0	2.66
GD McGrath	3	139	43	350	14	25.00	3–13	–	–	59.5	2.51
SK Warne	3	173.3	35	473	17	27.82	5–113	1	–	61.2	2.72
B Lee	3	105	27	314	9	34.88	3–77	–	–	70.0	2.99
JN Gillespie	1	34	11	80	2	40.00	2–23	–	–	102.0	2.35
ME Waugh	3	17	2	42	1	42.00	1–19	–	–	102.0	2.47
RT Ponting	3	1	0	11	0	–	–	–	–	–	11.00

South Africa Batting and Fielding

Name	Mat	Inn	NO	Runs	HS	Ave	SR	100	50	Ct	St
JH Kallis	3	6	1	245	99	49.00	41.38	–	2	4	–
G Kirsten	3	6	0	245	153	40.83	42.09	1	–	1	–
ND McKenzie	3	6	0	224	87	37.33	44.88	–	2	6	–
SM Pollock	3	6	2	128	61 *	32.00	55.41	–	1	2	–
MV Boucher	3	6	0	169	64	28.16	52.81	–	1	7	–
HH Gibbs	3	6	0	164	78	27.33	40.79	–	1	–	–
HH Dippenaar	3	6	0	130	74	21.66	48.87	–	1	–	–
JL Ontong	1	2	0	41	32	20.50	44.56	–	–	–	–
M Hayward	2	4	2	26	14	13.00	47.27	–	–	–	–
CW Henderson	3	6	0	65	30	10.83	33.16	–	–	2	–
L Klusener	2	4	0	47	22	11.75	47.95	–	–	1	–
M Ntini	1	2	0	13	9	6.50	27.08	–	–	1	–
N Boje	1	2	0	8	7	4.00	53.33	–	–	–	–
AA Donald	2	4	1	11	7	3.66	19.64	–	–	1	–

South Africa Bowling

Name	Mat	O	M	R	W	Ave	Best	5wi	10wm	SR	ER
N Boje	1	27.3	6	78	4	19.50	4–63	–	–	41.2	2.83
SM Pollock	3	112	27	312	8	39.00	3–84	–	–	84.0	2.78
L Klusener	2	25	5	82	2	41.00	2–44	–	–	75.0	3.28
M Hayward	2	67	6	249	5	49.80	3–108	–	–	80.4	3.71
AA Donald	2	65	11	238	4	59.50	3–103	–	–	97.5	3.66
CW Henderson	3	120.1	11	480	8	60.00	4–116	–	–	90.1	3.99
JH Kallis	3	70	7	266	4	66.50	3–45	–	–	105.0	3.80
M Ntini	1	27	10	77	0	–	–	–	–	–	2.85
JL Ontong	1	2	0	10	0	–	–	–	–	–	5.00

Notes

*	indicates not out
SR	indicates Strike Rate. For batting, the Strike Rate is determined by runs scored per 100 balls faced. For bowling, the Strike Rate is determined by wickets taken per balls bowled.
ER	indicates Economy Rate. The Economy Rate is determined by runs conceded per overs bowled.
4wi/5wi	indicates instances of a bowler taking four/five wickets in an innings.
10wm	indicates instances of a bowler taking 10 wickets in a match.

THE VB SERIES 2001–02, COMPETITION AVERAGES

Australia Batting and Fielding

Name	Mat	Inn	NO	Runs	HS	Ave	SR	100	50	Ct	St
MG Bevan	7	6	1	251	102 *	50.20	74.48	1	1	3	–
RJ Campbell	1	1	0	38	38	38.00	73.07	–	–	2	1
DR Martyn	8	8	2	226	104 *	37.66	63.12	1	–	2	–
RT Ponting	8	8	0	254	80	31.75	77.43	–	2	3	–
SR Waugh	8	7	1	187	62	31.16	69.00	–	1	3	–
JN Gillespie	5	3	2	29	15	29.00	60.41	–	–	–	–
ME Waugh	7	7	1	126	55 *	21.00	70.78	–	1	3	–
B Lee	5	5	1	79	51 *	19.75	101.28	–	1	–	–
AJ Bichel	6	3	1	37	17	18.50	75.51	–	–	3	–
AC Gilchrist	7	6	0	97	31	16.16	97.97	–	–	14	1
SK Warne	8	6	0	72	29	12.00	56.69	–	–	2	–
ML Hayden	2	2	0	20	10	10.00	38.46	–	–	1	–
IJ Harvey	3	3	0	23	12	7.66	48.93	–	–	1	–
GD McGrath	7	3	1	14	7	7.00	50.00	–	–	–	–
A Symonds	4	3	0	14	11	4.66	66.66	–	–	4	–
DS Lehmann	1	1	1	49	49 *	–	106.52	–	–	–	–
BA Williams	1	1	1	13	13 *	–	59.09	–	–	–	–

Australia Bowling

Name	Mat	O	M	R	W	Ave	Best	4wi	5wi	SR	ER
DS Lehmann	1	5	0	28	2	14.00	2–28	–	–	15.0	5.60
GD McGrath	7	69.4	10	226	14	16.14	4–30	1	–	29.8	3.24
DR Martyn	8	3	0	20	1	20.00	1–20	–	–	18.0	6.66
ME Waugh	7	11	0	46	2	23.00	2–38	–	–	33.0	4.18
AJ Bichel	6	46.3	2	206	8	25.75	5–19	–	1	34.8	4.43
B Lee	5	45.3	4	223	8	27.87	3–43	–	–	34.1	4.90
JN Gillespie	5	49	6	183	6	30.50	2–28	–	–	49.0	3.73
IJ Harvey	3	30	1	134	4	33.50	2–40	–	–	45.0	4.46
A Symonds	4	27	0	126	3	42.00	3–48	–	–	54.0	4.66
SK Warne	8	75	4	324	6	54.00	2–65	–	–	75.0	4.32
SR Waugh	8	10	0	59	0	–	–	–	–	–	5.90
BA Williams	1	10	2	31	0	–	–	–	–	–	3.10
MG Bevan	7	4	0	27	0	–	–	–	–	–	6.75

New Zealand Batting and Fielding

Name	Mat	Inn	NO	Runs	HS	Ave	SR	100	50	Ct	St
CL Cairns	9	9	2	314	102 *	44.85	93.17	1	2	2	–
CZ Harris	10	10	4	240	63 *	40.00	63.49	–	1	6	–
SP Fleming	9	9	0	309	85	34.33	65.60	–	3	5	–
CD McMillan	10	10	0	275	73	27.50	76.17	–	1	2	–
L Vincent	10	10	0	225	55	22.50	58.13	–	1	5	–
NJ Astle	6	6	0	122	95	20.33	62.88	–	1	4	–
AC Parore	10	9	3	109	36 *	18.16	64.11	–	–	15	–
BB McCullum	4	4	0	71	37	17.75	55.03	–	–	1	–
SB Styris	4	4	0	64	23	16.00	64.00	–	–	1	–
SE Bond	9	4	2	32	17 *	16.00	76.19	–	–	2	–
DJ Nash	4	3	0	45	24	15.00	78.94	–	–	1	–
AR Adams	4	4	1	37	13 *	12.33	115.62	–	–	1	–
DL Vettori	10	8	3	61	30	12.20	50.00	–	–	1	–
MH Richardson	4	4	0	42	26	10.50	43.29	–	–	1	–
JEC Franklin	7	5	1	18	9 *	4.50	45.00	–	–	3	–

New Zealand Bowling

Name	Mat	O	M	R	W	Ave	Best	4wi	5wi	SR	ER
SE Bond	9	82.2	10	344	21	16.38	5–25	2	1	23.5	4.17
DJ Nash	4	28	1	124	6	20.66	3–37	–	–	28.0	4.42
CL Cairns	9	70	5	319	12	26.58	3–42	–	–	35.0	4.55
AR Adams	4	36	0	174	4	43.50	2–33	–	–	54.0	4.83
CZ Harris	10	82.3	0	371	8	46.37	3–37	–	–	61.8	4.49
JEC Franklin	7	54	0	289	6	48.16	2–41	–	–	54.0	5.35
DL Vettori	10	83.1	1	368	7	52.57	2–36	–	–	71.2	4.42
SB Styris	4	13	0	74	0	–	–	–	–	–	5.69
NJ Astle	6	10	0	51	0	–	–	–	–	–	5.10
CD McMillan	10	7	0	39	0	–	–	–	–	–	5.57

South Africa Batting and Fielding

Name	Mat	Inn	NO	Runs	HS	Ave	SR	100	50	Ct	St
JN Rhodes	10	9	3	345	107 *	57.50	73.24	1	2	4	–
JH Kallis	8	8	2	322	104 *	53.66	70.61	1	2	5	–
MV Boucher	10	9	3	246	58	41.00	102.07	–	3	12	–
HH Dippenaar	6	6	1	185	79 *	37.00	61.46	–	1	3	–
HH Gibbs	10	10	0	293	89	29.30	69.10	–	1	6	–
SM Pollock	10	7	3	111	69 *	27.75	130.58	–	1	4	–
G Kirsten	10	10	0	265	97	26.50	63.24	–	1	4	–
ND McKenzie	6	6	0	150	68	25.00	63.55	–	1	1	–
L Klusener	7	5	1	64	25 *	16.00	98.46	–	–	4	–
S Elworthy	3	3	1	29	18	14.50	61.70	–	–	–	–
N Boje	8	2	1	14	13 *	14.00	33.33	–	–	1	–
JM Kemp	3	2	1	11	10 *	11.00	68.75	–	–	1	–
JL Ontong	2	1	0	4	4	4.00	44.44	–	–	4	–
CK Langeveldt	1	1	0	3	3	3.00	60.00	–	–	–	–
M Ntini	9	2	1	2	2 *	2.00	18.18	–	–	2	–
AA Donald	7	0	–	–	–	–	–	–	–	4	–

South Africa Bowling

Name	Mat	O	M	R	W	Ave	Best	4wi	5wi	SR	ER
M Ntini	9	81.2	7	338	14	24.14	5–31	–	1	34.8	4.15
AA Donald	7	65	5	301	12	25.08	3–29	–	–	32.5	4.63
SM Pollock	10	87.1	9	333	13	25.61	3–25	–	–	40.2	3.82
N Boje	8	58	0	205	8	25.62	4–31	1	–	43.5	3.53
L Klusener	7	44.4	0	238	9	26.44	2–27	–	–	29.7	5.32
JH Kallis	8	63.5	2	287	10	28.70	3–23	–	–	38.3	4.49
S Elworthy	3	20	1	100	3	33.33	2–53	–	–	40.0	5.00
JM Kemp	3	19	0	99	2	49.50	2–50	–	–	57.0	5.21
JL Ontong	2	7	0	34	0	–	–	–	–	–	4.85
CK Langeveldt	1	5	0	31	0	–	–	–	–	–	6.20

VB SERIES 2001–02 FINAL COMPETITION TABLE

Team	Played	Won	Lost	NR	Tied	BP	Points	NRR
South Africa	8	4	4	–	–	2	18	-0.040
New Zealand	8	4	4	–	–	1	17	-0.154
Australia	8	4	4	–	–	1	17	+0.186

Notes

- NR indicates No Result
- BP indicates Bonus Points
- NRR indicates Net Run-rate
- A bonus point was awarded when a team achieved a run rate of 1.25 times that of their opponents in a match.
- New Zealand qualified for the final because they won three of their four matches against Australia. For a situation where teams finished level on the final table, the order of tiebreakers was as follows:
  1. The team with the most number of wins
  2. The team with the most number of wins over the other team(s) with whom they finished level.
  3. The team with the highest number of bonus points
  4. The team with the highest net run-rate.

THE AUSTRALIANS IN SOUTH AFRICA 2001–02, TEST AVERAGES

Australia Batting and Fielding

Name	Mat	Inn	NO	Runs	HS	Ave	SR	100	50	Ct	St
AC Gilchrist	3	5	2	473	204 *	157.66	99.78	2	1	13	1
RT Ponting	3	5	1	309	100 *	77.25	76.48	1	1	4	–
ML Hayden	3	5	0	309	122	61.80	65.88	1	2	4	–
ME Waugh	3	5	0	169	53	33.80	56.71	–	1	6	–
SK Warne	3	5	1	129	63	32.25	96.26	–	1	5	–
JL Langer	3	5	0	152	58	30.40	93.82	–	1	2	–
DR Martyn	3	5	0	146	133	29.20	55.30	1	–	3	–
SR Waugh	3	5	0	95	42	19.00	40.25	–	–	1	–
B Lee	3	4	2	27	23 *	13.50	41.53	–	–	1	–
GD McGrath	3	3	1	6	4 *	3.00	26.08	–	–	1	–
JN Gillespie	3	3	0	4	3	1.33	7.01	–	–	1	–

Australia Bowling

Name	Mat	O	M	R	W	Ave	Best	5wi	10wm	SR	ER
GD McGrath	3	110.3	36	227	12	18.91	5–21	1	–	55.2	2.05
SK Warne	3	162	38	442	20	22.10	6–161	1	–	48.6	2.72
JN Gillespie	3	92	28	287	8	35.87	3–52	–	–	69.0	3.11
ME Waugh	3	21.5	4	78	2	39.00	2–43	–	–	65.5	3.57
B Lee	3	95.2	10	416	10	41.60	4–82	–	–	57.2	4.36
SR Waugh	3	3	0	16	0	–	–	–	–	–	5.33
DR Martyn	3	4	0	15	0	–	–	–	–	–	3.75

South Africa Batting and Fielding

Name	Mat	Inn	NO	Runs	HS	Ave	SR	100	50	Ct	St
AJ Hall	2	3	1	97	70	48.50	49.23	–	1	1	–
HH Gibbs	3	6	0	287	104	47.83	57.28	1	1	2	–
ND McKenzie	3	6	1	191	99	38.20	44.41	–	1	4	–
JH Kallis	3	6	1	184	73	36.80	55.92	–	2	4	–
G Kirsten	3	6	0	192	87	32.00	48.24	–	2	2	–
PR Adams	2	3	1	64	35	32.00	40.25	–	–	–	–
GC Smith	2	4	0	114	68	28.50	46.72	–	1	2	–
AG Prince	3	6	0	155	49	25.83	41.22	–	–	2	–
MV Boucher	3	6	1	95	37	19.00	57.57	–	–	13	–
M Ntini	3	5	0	48	14	9.60	72.72	–	–	–	–
D Pretorius	1	2	1	5	5 *	5.00	71.42	–	–	–	–
A Nel	1	2	0	7	7	3.50	38.88	–	–	–	–
AA Donald	1	2	1	3	3 *	3.00	25.00	–	–	–	–
N Boje	1	2	0	5	5	2.50	27.77	–	–	–	–
HH Dippenaar	1	2	0	3	2	1.50	9.09	–	–	–	–
DJ Terbrugge	1	1	0	0	0	0.00	0.00	–	–	1	–

South Africa Bowling

Name	Mat	O	M	R	W	Ave	Best	5wi	10wm	SR	ER
DJ Terbrugge	1	20	3	82	4	20.50	2–21	–	–	30.0	4.10
PR Adams	2	63.1	1	290	10	29.00	4–102	–	–	37.9	4.59
JH Kallis	3	88	9	373	11	33.90	3–29	–	–	48.0	4.23
M Ntini	3	116.5	22	459	11	41.72	4–93	–	–	63.7	3.92
A Nel	1	30.4	6	121	2	60.50	2–121	–	–	92.0	3.94
AA Donald	1	15.2	2	72	1	72.00	1–72	–	–	92.0	4.69
AJ Hall	2	27.1	4	108	1	108.00	1–35	–	–	163.0	3.97
D Pretorius	1	25	6	132	1	132.00	1–60	–	–	150.0	5.28
N Boje	1	35	4	153	1	153.00	1–153	–	–	210.0	4.37
ND McKenzie	3	8	0	50	0	–	–	–	–	–	6.25

THE AUSTRALIANS IN SOUTH AFRICA 2001–02, TOUR AVERAGES

Batting and Fielding

Name	Mat	Inn	NO	Runs	HS	Ave	SR	100	50	Ct	St
AC Gilchrist	5	8	3	545	204*	109.00	93.16	2	2	20	1
RT Ponting	5	7	1	469	120	78.16	78.29	2	1	5	–
DS Lehmann	1	1	0	60	60	60.00	63.82	–	1	–	–
ML Hayden	4	7	0	366	122	52.28	64.55	1	2	5	–
ME Waugh	5	7	0	341	110	48.71	67.25	1	2	8	–
JL Langer	5	8	0	370	161	46.25	66.66	1	1	3	–
SR Waugh	5	7	1	201	102*	33.50	51.93	1	–	2	–
DR Martyn	4	7	1	157	133	26.16	51.64	1	–	3	–
SK Warne	4	6	1	129	63	25.80	93.47	–	1	5	–
AJ Bichel	1	1	0	9	9	9.00	75.00	–	–	–	–
JN Gillespie	5	5	1	24	15	6.00	22.01	–	–	2	–
B Lee	5	7	2	33	23*	6.60	40.24	–	–	2	–
GD McGrath	4	3	1	6	4*	3.00	26.08	–	–	1	–
SR Watson	1	1	1	100	100*	–	103.09	1	–	–	–
SCG MacGill	1	1	1	0	0*	–	0.00	–	–	1	–

Bowling

Name	Mat	O	M	R	W	Ave	Best	5wi	10wm	SR	ER
GD McGrath	4	125.3	45	244	17	14.35	5–17	2	–	44.2	1.94
SR Watson	1	22	5	60	3	20.00	2–40	–	–	44.0	2.72
SK Warne	4	178	40	501	22	22.77	6–161	1	–	48.5	2.81
AJ Bichel	1	27.3	2	123	5	24.60	3–41	–	–	33.0	4.47
B Lee	5	137.2	16	540	18	30.00	4–37	–	–	45.7	3.93
JN Gillespie	5	132	42	387	10	38.70	3–52	–	–	79.2	2.93
SCG MacGill	1	50.3	9	208	5	41.60	4–114	–	–	60.6	4.11
ME Waugh	5	25.5	5	86	2	43.00	2–43	–	–	77.5	3.32
DR Martyn	4	8	2	22	0	–	–	–	–	–	2.75
SR Waugh	5	3	0	16	0	–	–	–	–	–	5.33

ICC TEST CHAMPIONSHIP TABLE (AS AT 9 SEPTEMBER 2002)

Rank	Team	Played	Won	Lost	Drawn	Points	Average
1	Australia	13	9	2	2	20	1.54
2	South Africa	16	11	3	2	24	1.50
3	New Zealand	17	8	5	4	20	1.18
4	Sri Lanka	16	8	6	2	18	1.13
5	England	16	6	6	4	16	1.00
6	West Indies	15	6	8	1	13	0.87
7	India	14	4	6	4	12	0.86
8	Pakistan	16	4	7	5	13	0.81
9	Zimbabwe	16	3	11	2	8	0.50
–	Bangladesh	5	–	5	–	0	–

Notes
- The Test Championship table — based on a concept that had originally been developed by *Wisden* — was formally introduced in May 2001, and is currently based on series that started during or after May 1996. From this starting point, more recently played series between two teams replace older ones as the series to be counted for the purpose of the table. Home series replace home series; away series replace away series. Thus, for example, the result of the 2002–03 Ashes series in Australia will replace the result of the previous Ashes series played in Australia, the 1998–99 series.
- Teams receive two points for a series win, one for a series draw, none for a series loss.
- Teams are currently ranked on average (number of points won divided by number of series played). It is intended that the table will be based on a straight points system once every team has played each other home and away in the period from May 1996. This is scheduled to occur in 2005.
- Only series consisting of two Tests or more are counted.
- If, for any reason, a scheduled series is not played or completed, no points are awarded. This ruling was made to provide an incentive for teams to fulfil all fixtures.
- The leading team holds the ICC Test Championship trophy. The trophy automatically passes from leader to leader.
- If two sides become tied at the top of the table, the holder retains the trophy.
- Australia would lose its place at the top of the table if it did not win its October 2002 away series against Pakistan.

AUSTRALIAN CRICKETERS WHO PLAYED UNDER STEVE WAUGH'S CAPTAINCY, 1999–2002

From the time Steve Waugh was first appointed Australia's Test captain, for the West Indies tour of 1999, through to the conclusion of the 2001–02 Test series in South Africa, Australia played 39 Tests (for 27 wins, seven losses and five draws) and 77 one-day internationals (54 wins, 19 losses, three ties and one no result). Waugh led Australia in 37 of those Tests, with Adam Gilchrist in charge of the other two, and in 74 of the one-day internationals (ODIs), with Gilchrist deputising on three occasions.

In this period — from the first Test against the West Indies in March 1999 through to the third Test against South Africa in March 2002 — 23 players appeared for Australia in Test cricket, as follows:

Tests	Player	Tests	Player
39	Mark Waugh, Glenn McGrath	15	Greg Blewett
37	Steve Waugh	12	Colin Miller
35	Justin Langer	10	Damien Fleming
34	Ricky Ponting	9	Stuart MacGill
33	Shane Warne	8	Ian Healy
31	Adam Gilchrist	3	Andy Bichel, Matthew Elliott,
29	Michael Slater		Michael Kasprowicz
23	Jason Gillespie, Matthew Hayden	2	Scott Muller
21	Brett Lee	1	Adam Dale, Simon Katich
18	Damien Martyn		

In a similar period — from the first ODI against the West Indies in April 1999 through to the end of the VB Series in 2001–02 — 27 players appeared for Australia in ODI cricket:

ODIs	Player	ODIs	Player
75	Adam Gilchrist	29	Shane Lee
74	Michael Bevan, Steve Waugh	27	Ian Harvey
70	Mark Waugh	18	Tom Moody
67	Shane Warne	16	Matthew Hayden
63	Ricky Ponting	15	Jason Gillespie
62	Glenn McGrath	9	Nathan Bracken, Paul Reiffel
56	Damien Martyn	7	Brendon Julian
47	Andrew Symonds	6	Andy Bichel, Adam Dale
44	Damien Fleming	3	Stuart MacGill
34	Brett Lee	1	Ryan Campbell, Brad Haddin,
32	Darren Lehmann		Simon Katich, Brad Williams

Notes
1. Simon Katich is the only cricketer in the table of ODI appearances above not to play in a ODI under Steve Waugh's captaincy. Katich also managed to make his one Test appearance when Waugh was unavailable — he replaced the injured captain for the fourth Test of the 2001 Ashes series.
2. Steve Waugh led Australia in 32 one-day internationals before the 1999 West Indies tour, starting with the final match of the Australians' 1997 tour of South Africa. Cricketers who played under Waugh's captaincy in ODIs in this period, but not during or after the '99 Windies tour, were Michael Di Venuto, Matthew Elliott, Justin Langer, Stuart Law, Jimmy Maher, Greg Blewett, Ian Healy, Gavin Robertson, Michael Kasprowicz, Paul Wilson and Brad Young.